FREEDOM FROM ALLERGY

COOKBOOK

Wheat, Yeast and Milk Free Recipes

RON GREENBERG, M.D.
ANGELA NORI

BLUE POPPY PRESS

Before making major changes in your diet, contact your doctor.

Typesetting: The Typeworks
Cover painting: Rosalie Rupp Prussing
Cover design: Bob English
Back cover photo: Harlan Lahti
Printed in Canada

Copyright 1991 — Ronald Greenberg & Angela Nori
Third Edition
ISBN 0-88925-905-4

Greenberg, Ron, 1949-
    Freedom from allergy cookbook

    First ed. published under title: So what can I eat, eh?
    Includes index.

    1. Food allergy — Diet therapy — Recipes.
I. Nori, Angela,   II. Title.
RC588.D53G74 1988   641.5'631   C88-091518-8

Blue Poppy Press
212-2678 West Broadway
Vancouver, B.C. Canada V6K 2G3

Table of Contents

How to Use this Book

Before you use any of the recipes in this book, stop! You will find that cooking and eating a wide variety of foods will be much easier if you first read all of the sections before the recipes.

Introduction

If you have just discovered that you have food allergies, relax. It is likely that many of the foods you are avoiding may well be reintroduced over the next months. You will also be better able to deal with the dietary changes if you are optimistic, calm and well prepared. You are avoiding these foods to rest your immune system. It is helpful also to rest your mind. Instead of maintaining a sense of deprivation, you could develop a positive sense of helping yourself to greater health by staying away from things that adversely affect you. By changing the foods that you eat, you are bringing out your basic healthiness that is being obscured by what you have been inadvertently doing to yourself. Be flexible - let yourself acquire a taste for new foods and new patterns of choosing foods.

Your change of diet may pose many new options. Beyond the question of "What can I eat?" is the question, "How do I prepare it?" This book is designed for people who know or suspect that they are sensitive to one or more foods and wish to avoid them. You will find information on what foods to avoid, what foods to substitute and how to prepare them. We will also show you how to rotate your foods and why you might want to do that. After reading and using this book, you can be well-nourished, eat happily and enjoy the foods that enhance your health and well being.

You may notice that the recipes are low in salt and fat. They are very suitable for people trying to lower their cholesterol level. You will be introduced to many delicious foods that you might otherwise never discover. Because we are both busy and like to eat we developed these recipes so that you can prepare them with a minimum of fuss and time. We know that people with allergies get hungry too.

Understanding Allergy

What is an allergy?

An allergy is an adverse response to a substance e.g. dust, pollen, milk, carrot, that normally would not cause a problem in a non-allergic individual. Allergic reactions are caused by events within your immune system; reactions to foods that are caused by over-eating are not allergies; reactions caused by digestive problems or food-poisoning are not allergies. Sometimes it is difficult to distinguish a true allergic reaction from a problem caused by a different mechanism because the resulting symptoms may be the same.

The immune system mechanisms that result in allergy symptoms are in many ways similar to the ways that our bodies control infections. Our white blood cells are stimulated by infection to reproduce and to produce certain types of cells and chemicals to kill bacteria and viruses. Similarly, the presence of foods to which we may be allergic causes some white blood cells called lymphocytes, to release certain proteins called immunoglobulins. These immunoglobulins may react with other cells in the tissues of our nose, lungs, skin or gut to release chemicals such as histamine. It is these chemicals, when they react with parts of our body, that initiate all the symptoms that we call allergic reactions.

Why do I have allergies?

If you are allergic to anything, you probably inherited the predisposition to allergy from your parents. If both of your parents have allergies, then you have at least a 75% chance of developing allergies some time in your life. Many people only realize that they have a family history of allergy after they discover their own allergy and start checking other family members. Often allergies will appear, relatively late in life, to substances that apparently had been well tolerated for years. However, if you think back you may be able to trace the subtle effects allergies have had in your life for many years.

The particular foods to which you become allergic depend on what exposures you have had. For example, North Americans are frequently reactive to milk and wheat while Orientals eating traditional foods are often reactive to rice and soybean. Sometimes the appearance of allergies follows an infection. Sometimes it seems to follow exposure to chemicals. It is the repeated use of specific foods that determines to which foods you will probably become allergic. Recent studies indicate that the number of people with allergies and their severity is increasing and that chemical pollution of our air, food and water may play a role in the development of allergies. Generally, urban populations have more problems than rural. Any food or food additive can be allergenic. The most common food allergens in the Western diet are: Milk, wheat, yeast, corn, citrus, egg, soy, peanut, shellfish and chocolate.

What can allergies do to me?
There is a wide range of problems and symptoms that result from food allergy. However, food allergy is certainly not the cause of all of these problems in everyone. Starting in the mouth, allergies sometimes cause mouth ulcers, swelling of the tongue and throat, stomach ulcers, nausea, vomiting, indigestion, pains that mimic gall-bladder attacks, Crohn's disease, irritable bowel syndrome, ulcerative colitis, diarrhea, constipation. Starting from the nose and eyes, there are runny noses, congested noses, recurrent ear infections, sore throat, mucus in the throat, chronic coughs and asthma. On the skin, eczema, hives, occasionally acne and psoriasis. Joint aches and pains, arthritis and muscle aches. Migraine headaches, chronic fatigue and sleepiness. Anxiety, depression, panic attack, irritability, behavioral problems, and insomnia. Sometimes pre-menstrual symptoms, nausea of pregnancy and vaginal discharges. The list goes on and on. It seems that almost any long term problem can be caused by food allergy. Many people with persistent symptoms, who have been from doctor to doctor without relief or who have been told that their problems are in their heads, have problems caused by food allergy. Most people

who have "hypoglycemic" symptoms, or suspect they have the 'Candida Yeast syndrome,' are allergic to food. Many illnesses not directly caused by allergies can be worsened by allergic reaction, such as chronic bronchitis—emphysema.

The Candida or yeast syndrome deserves special mention. Many people having read or heard about it believe that they have an infection of yeast throughout their bodies. In fact some people do carry a large number of these yeast cells in their lower bowel or vagina, though not the rest of their bodies, to which they may be allergic, and these people require special treatment. However, the majority of these people have food allergies. The special diet they have been following is an excellent food allergy avoidance diet and for that reason, going on the diet usually prescribed seems to help a lot of these people. They have eliminated their major allergens and this rather than the use of special nutrient supplements is what helps the majority.

How is food allergy different?

In order to control your allergies, it is useful to understand the nature of food allergy. Food allergies can appear in two different ways; either as fixed or as cyclical reactions. Cyclical food allergies can appear as either masked or unmasked reactions. Allergies to airborne inhalants such as dust mite, pollens or animal danders are similar to fixed food allergies.

1. Fixed food allergy

Fixed food allergies are the type of reactions that some people have every time that they eat or even breathe the fumes of a small amount of a particular food. Often these reactions are strong and potentially dangerous. They appear soon after contact with the food. This type of allergic reaction is a lifelong pattern and is unlikely to disappear. Most people have no problem identifying a fixed food allergy reaction. Fixed food allergens will always need to be avoided. People with a fixed food reaction to a fish should be cautious with all fish. Similarly, be cautious with all nuts if one is very reactive.

2. Cyclical food allergy - Why do food allergies seem to come and go?

Cyclical food reactions follow a different pattern. If you have this

3

type of allergic response you may notice a reaction but not each time you eat the food. Your reactions may range from being quite weak to being more severe, but are seldom dangerous. In fact, many times you may not notice your reaction at all. When noticed, the reaction may take place many hours after you ate the food. The presence and strength of a cyclical food allergy depends on how much you eat and how often you eat a particular food. For example, drinking one glass of milk once a week may not cause you any noticeable reaction. However, drinking two or three glasses at once (increased amount) or drinking one glass two or three days in a row (increased frequency) may result in a noticeable allergic reaction, either soon after or many hours after drinking the milk. With constant exposure to an allergy, acute symptoms may temporarily disappear or become chronic as your body tries to adapt to the exposure.

3. Food addiction - Why is it always my favourite foods?

If a reaction occurs soon after eating a food and you can attribute it to the food, that is called an unmasked reaction. If the reaction occurs many hours after eating the food and you do not make the connection, the reaction is said to be masked. Masked cyclical reactions are probably the most common type. They are the reason many people do not realize that their health problems are related to foods. Repeated use of a food to which you are reacting can result in symptoms that become chronic and do not necessarily occur or worsen at the time that you eat the food. Because some people feel slightly stimulated - frequently without noticing it - after eating a reactive food, they may come to crave the food that is giving them delayed adverse symptoms. Some people may also feel poorly for a couple of days when they avoid a reactive food. As a result, they may think they need the food to stay healthy, although it is more likely to be the source of their health problems. These stimulatory and withdrawal patterns have led to the use of the phrase, "food addiction" to describe this pattern of food reactivity. These patterns lead to craving, and over-eating or over-drinking specific foods. Often we may think that a food that we crave is good for us. Obviously this is not true for people who crave salt, sugar, coffee, alcohol and tobacco. Indeed, it is frequently the foods that we crave that are the causes of many of our reactions. Simply giving up those foods for a few weeks can often have a remarkably beneficial effect.

4

4. Unmasking food allergy

To unmask a food allergy it is necessary to completely avoid the suspected food for four or five days. This includes hidden sources of the food in prepared or restaurant meals. Eating the food may then result in a noticeable and unexpected reaction. The nature of cyclical food allergy is such that if you avoid the allergen for a sufficiently long period, your reaction to the food may disappear. This is one reason not to despair if you are allergic to your favourite food. If you are patient, you will probably be able to eat that food again without reacting to it.

5. How do I determine my specific allergies?

There are many different types of allergy tests being used. None are perfect. Some are better, some are very unreliable. The most reliable approach is to combine the results of skin testing, which probably gives a slight over-reading of your allergies with a food avoidance and challenge procedure. After staying away from a suspected food for three weeks, you could eat a portion of that food to see if that challenge reproduces your symptoms. Do not however challenge a food to which you have had a strong or fixed food allergy. If you do not react, that would indicate either that you have a cyclical food allergy to that item and the allergy has disappeared, or the test was a false positive. If you do react to the tested food, stay off it for another three to six months and try again.

There are many allergy tests with low or unknown reliability. A blood test called RAST measures food specific immunoglobins but is most helpful in determining strong fixed food reactions and monitoring the effect of allergy injections.

Of course you can always look at the overall pattern of your usual diet and avoid the most common food allergens, i.e. use an elimination diet. What you eliminate depends on where you live and therefore what you eat. In Canada the foods to initially avoid would be wheat, milk, yeast, apple, orange, onion, coffee and corn. In the U.S. corn is a very, very frequent allergen. You could also avoid any food you eat more than two times weekly. If you feel better after two to three weeks then try to challenge them one at a time and see if there is a reaction. Of course the precaution above still applies: do not challenge a food to which you have had a strong or fixed food reaction.

Working With Your Allergies

What can I do about my allergies?

There are only a few ways to solve the problems caused by food allergies. Allergy shots, called immunotherapy by physicians, often work very well for airborne inhalant allergies such as pollens. However, they do not work as reliably for food allergies. There are reports of people deriving benefits from food immunotherapy but the percentage of people who have had good results is not as high as would be hoped. There are occasionally people who have various endocrine (hormonal) or other problems who find that their allergies improve when these problems are corrected. Sometimes the use of adequate amounts and appropriate types of nutritional supplements can be of benefit. It is of great value to stop smoking since smoking can increase the number and severity of allergies and infections. Controlling allergies to inhalant allergens by avoidance or immunotherapy can sometimes increase your overall tolerance for reactive foods. Reducing the amount of stress in your life can also help a great deal. Frequently, allergies become much worse when people are under emotional stress from jobs or relationships, and then improve when the stress is reduced. This is probably the reason some people, including doctors, will tell you that allergies are all in your head. Reducing stress through regular moderate exercise, relaxation techniques or meditation can be of enormous value. Minimizing exposure to bothersome chemicals such as perfume, tobacco, exhaust fumes and plastic smells may be useful.

However, probably the most important think that you can do to control your allergy symptoms is to avoid the allergenic foods that you have been eating. The rest of this book has been written to help you to do just that.

What is a Rotation Plan?

The Rotation Plan (see page 16) is a pattern for eating a wide range of different foods, organized so that you do not keep eating the same foods day after day. The Rotation Plan has several important advantages for you. First, when you start avoiding a reactive food, you may be tempted to replace it with just one other food. As a result of the repeated use of this other food, you may become reactive to it as well. Similarly, after avoiding the reactive food for several months, you may stop reacting to it but if you start eating it every day again, you may once more become sensitive to it. Second, you probably have not been tested to every food that you eat. You may also have discovered that some foods give you only minor problems when you eat them, especially if you eat them infrequently. You can prevent further problems from arising and perhaps control present minor problems by rotating your foods. This means that any food will be eaten only once in four days and avoided for the next three days. Occasionally, people find that they are only sensitive to one category of food such as meats or grains or fruits. In this situation, it may be necessary to only rotate that one category. It is usually helpful to rotate the grain group.

The Rotation Plan can also be used to develop alternatives to specific foods you need to avoid. Look across the columns for ideas for alternative foods in each category.

There are two ways to use the Rotation Plan. You can start each day of rotation with breakfast and eat the allowed foods on that day until you go to bed. Alternatively, you could start the rotation day with your evening meal and continue it until lunch or coffee break the next afternoon. This would allow you to use supper leftovers for breakfast or lunch.

The numbers beside the food names on the Rotation Plan page refer to the biological family to which the food belongs. All foods with the same number, e.g. soy and peanut - 14, belong to the same family and should always be eaten on the same day. You may find it more convenient to eat a certain food on a different day than the one to which it is assigned. In that case you should move all the foods with the same number to that new day. You may eat as many of the foods from a given day, from any of the categories that you wish, except the foods to which you are sensitive. If you wish to eat a food from another rotation day, it will not cause a problem if you have not eaten it for at least the previous 3 days and avoid it for at least the next 3 days. Some people feel better if they eat a food only once in the day. To others this does not matter. This rotation plan was arbitrarily created with a view to providing foods from all the food categories on each day. Eventually you may want to create your own rotation pattern based on your food preferences. Sometimes foods within a family are cross-reactive. For example, if you are sensitive to tomato, you may also react to green pepper and eggplant. While you do not need to avoid all the foods in a family, if you are reactive to one member of a family, you should be watchful for any reactions from eating other members of the family. Most people who react to wheat also react to rye and barley; they should also be avoided. Yogurt, cheese and ice cream almost always will be reactive foods if you are milk sensitive. Most people, 70% or more, who react to cow's milk will also react to goat's milk. It too should be avoided initially. Other foods that often cross-react are celery and carrot, celery and apple, carrot and apple, eggs and all forms of poultry. Less commonly soy and peanut, tomato and green pepper, apple and pear, melon and cucumber, milk and beef may cross react. Occasionally people reactive to wheat will react also to all of the grains including rye, barley, oat, rice, wild rice, cane sugar, bamboo shoots, millet and corn. Orange and other citrus fruit cross-react. Pineapple and tomato are not citrus fruits.

What will happen when I go on my avoidance plan?

When you start, it is important that you carefully avoid all of the foods, that your doctor has advised or you suspect, for an initial period of one to three months as he or she has indicated. The goal of this initial stage is to see how much better you can feel when your sensitivities are well controlled. During the first few days of this period a very small number of people may experience withdrawal reactions from their reactive foods. These are often minor, but foods like coffee and tea can produce stronger withdrawal reactions. You should consult your doctor if the reactions are too unpleasant. When you begin to avoid your specific foods it may take just a day or two, or up to two or three months before you start to feel better. If after four to six weeks there has been no improvement and you have been carefully following your avoidance programme, you should see your doctor for reappraisal.

9

The length of time that you can expect to have to avoid your specific foods is variable. Fixed food allergens will probably have to be avoided forever. When you are feeling well, your doctor may ask you to challenge your cyclical food allergens one by one at home to see if you have developed tolerance to any of them. You may find that after several weeks or months you may become tolerant to most or all of these foods. If you decide to eat these tolerated foods again you should rotate them or you may find that eventually you will again start to react to them and feel ill. You may mistakenly assume that your food allergies are gone forever after a period of avoidance and reintroduction of those foods. However, if your old problems return, remember that it might be your food sensitivities becoming active again, particularly if you have not been rotating.

What other dietary changes will I need to make?

While you are exploring your new way of eating, you should also be careful about several other non-specific factors. Many people are allergic to sugar, coffee and tea. These substances can also cause problems, by non-allergic mechanisms, through their metabolic effects on your body. Even though you may not have been allergy tested for them, they should be avoided when you start your new eating pattern.

Alcohol causes problems for many people. It contains allergens such as grains and yeast. By affecting your bowel lining it can speed the absorption of food allergens and result in faster, more severe reactions to any food allergens. It can cause non-allergic, metabolic problems. It is best to avoid alcohol.

As mentioned before, smoking can increase the severity and number of your allergies. It should also be completely stopped. Some people are reactive to food additives. The worst of these are food colourings such as tartarzine, food flavourings, MSG and sulphur dioxide. They may seem to be in all foods, but if you read labels carefully and prepare as many foods as possible yourself, you will find avoidance to be much less difficult. (See page 34.)

When you shop, read labels carefully. You will find many surprises. You may find having a small freezer very helpful for keeping enough different foods available. Freezing your own fruits, berries, etc. gives you complete control of their content and can save a lot of money. You can also freeze fish, meats, muffins or vegetables.

How can I eat out while avoiding my allergens?

1. Friends

If you have been invited out for a meal, you could call before and mention your sensitivities and tactfully offer some simple ideas for a tolerated meal such as a meat or fish simply cooked or a salad with the dressing left on the table for the guests to add their own. You could also offer to bring one or two things, that you can tolerate, to complement your friend's meal. If alcohol is being served, ask for mineral water or club soda. If you have not made any advance arrangements you could tell your friends when you arrive that you have specific food allergies and ask that they not be offended if you do not eat certain things.

2. Restaurants

Salad bars or buffet restaurants allow you to see what they have before you serve yourself. Always ask if what you have ordered from a menu contains foods to which you are allergic. If, when the food arrives, it contains something that you did not expect, you would be completely justified in sending it back, especially if you could not separate the offending item from the rest of your meal. It often helps if you over-emphasize to the waiter the horrible things that will happen in the restaurant if he or she misleads you.

3. Lunch

The recipes contain many ideas for lunch. Many things that you normally eat for lunch or dinner can be adapted to suit your sensitivities. If you usually take sandwiches with you, place an increased amount of the filling into a container, perhaps making it into a salad, and eat that, omitting the bread, with an appropriate muffin, leftover pancake or unyeasted bread from the recipes. Use dinner leftovers in the same way. You could take rice cakes, tortillas or oatcakes which are available at supermarkets or health food stores. It is helpful to make several types of muffins in advance and keep them frozen until you need them. (Tag foods in your freezer with coloured labels to distinguish the rotation diet days.) Children at school might be given extra muffins, etc. so that they can share their unique meals with their friends without needing to trade for allergenic foods.

11

Can I cheat on my avoidance?

During the initial period of avoidance of your allergic foods you should not eat any of those foods, otherwise you may not derive any benefit from the avoidance period. Later, if you must eat any of these foods you could choose just one day in the week for all of your indulgences. That way if you react you will feel poorly for only a day or so. If you lapse a little every day you may find yourself feeling poorly most days of the week since reactions can last for several days.

How to Use the Recipes

You will find in the recipes ideas on how to cook and eat regardless of what your sensitivities are. The tabbed pages contain recipes that are matched to the Rotation Plan days. Recipes on the white pages avoid wheat, yeast and milk, but do not necessarily follow the rotation pattern. When using the recipes you will notice that many items are listed as optional. For example, you may see egg, sweetener or a milk alternative in the recipes. Often you can just leave them out, if you are sensitive, correcting for the liquid by adding water. Alternatively, you could check the lists of egg replacers, sugar alternatives or dairy alternatives listed in the following pages. Use one that you can tolerate and that seems appropriate to the recipe. Some recipes will give you suggestions for alternatives. If you are sensitive to a major ingredient in a recipe, you can find an alternative for it. Not all alternatives are appropriate in all recipes and some may require the slight modification of liquid or other factors in a recipe. If you are not sensitive to eggs or milk you may add these to some recipes to change their taste or texture. Salt and sweeteners are optional in all recipes and may be omitted. The taste for salt is learned and quickly disappears when not used for a few weeks. Recent research indicates that asthma may be much improved by avoiding salt.

The quality of many flours used in these recipes will vary between manufacturers. Storage will also alter them. Therefore, when adding liquid in a recipe you may have to be flexible to achieve a proper batter consistency. Some flours go rancid easily. It is probably best to store small amounts in your refrigerator or freezer.

Sugar or sweeteners is optional in all recipes and may be left out.

Nutritional Needs

While on an avoidance diet you must be careful to eat enough protein, calories, vitamins and minerals. In the next few pages you will find lists of the protein and calcium content of foods; calculate your needs and your weekly intake, and eat enough of what you need. There is also a list of vitamins and minerals, and the foods in which they are found. If you are uncertain about whether you are getting enough of any nutrient, take a supplement and/or speak to your doctor.

Calories

If you are concerned about not getting enough calories in your diet and losing weight, the following list and the starchy vegetable list on the Rotation Plan page will be helpful. The number of calories in one slice of bread is roughly equivalent to any of

½ cup of raw or cooked carrots, broccoli, beets, brussel sprouts, parsnips, peas, squash, turnips, corn or potato;

⅓ cup of cooked oats, rice, cornmeal, millet, sweet potato, beans, etc.;

¼ pound of tofu;

¾ tablespoon of nut butter.

The recipes in the cookbook for muffins, pancakes and unyeasted breads are also good alternatives for bread.

Dietary Fibre

If you eliminate wheat or other grains, you may find yourself becoming constipated. This can be avoided by using extra dietary fibre from new sources. On day one of the rotation you can use psyllium seed husk. this is available from health food stores. Take one teaspoon, two times daily by mixing it in a glass of cool water or juice. Follow that with a second glass of water. On day two, use one tablespoon of flax seeds. Either let it sit for several hours in a glass of water and then drink the thick fluid that develops or grind it, freshly each time as it goes rancid, in a blender or coffee mill and drink with two glasses of water as with the psyllium. On day three, sprinkle rice bran onto your food as you would wheat bran or mix ¼ cup with water and spoon or drink the mixture. On day four, use oat bran. Cook up ¼–½ cup with water as you would porridge. It is available at super-markets. You may need to adjust the amounts of any of these forms of roughage to suit your particular needs. All of these are available at health food and specialty stores.

Beverages

You probably have been asked to avoid coffee and tea. If you are yeast sensitive you may have been asked to avoid canned, frozen and especially boxed juices. You may be wondering what is left to drink. Water in its many forms is an ideal beverage. There are occasional reports of people who react to tap or bottled water, but these are uncommon. If you are not accustomed to drinking water, you could explore the use of carbonated mineral waters or club soda initially. Tap water taken very cold can be very refreshing. Taken hot after boiling, it can be as soothing as a cup of tea or coffee, especially in the morning, after meals or on cold days. See the 'Drink' section of the Rotation Plan for ideas for herbal teas. If you have a juicer, make your own fruit and vegetable juices. Some juices can be made in a blender by pressing and filtering the pulp after blending. This often works well after cooking the fruit.

Plan your meals in advance so that you have the food that you will need on hand when you want it. Discuss your diet with your housemates. Ask for their support and encouragement. You can expect a five-pound weight loss initially. This usually returns when you have adapted to your new eating pattern. Unless you are overweight, do not let your weight drop further without speaking to your doctor. The weight loss is usually caused by not eating enough new foods to replace the foods that you are avoiding.

Mark your favourite recipes and any changes you make to them.

Record new recipes or adaptations of the recipes. It is often useful during the first few weeks to record everything that you eat and how you feel during the day.

You are working on feeling better by effectively using this eating plan and although it would be a mistake to attribute every untoward event in your life to allergy, isn't it nice to be gaining a sense of control over your life?

FOUR DAY ROTARY DIVERSIFIED PLAN

	DAY ONE	DAY TWO	DAY THREE	DAY FOUR
FISH	80. Sturgeon 81. Shark 82. Anchovy, Shad 83. Salmon, Trout 84. Lake White Fish	85. Smelt 86. Pike 87. Carp 88. Cod, Haddock 89. Mullet	90. Herring, Sardine 91. Red Snapper 92. Yellow Perch 93. Blue Fish 94. Amberjack	95. Porgy 96. Mackerel, Tuna 97. Flounder, Halibut 98. Sole 99. Ocean Perch
MEAT	63. Beef, Veal, Cow cheese, Buffalo 58. Mollusks:Clam, Abalone, Mussel, Squid, Octopus	62. a) Chicken, Quail, Pheasant, Egg 62. b) Duck, Goose c) Turkey 62. d) Squab (Pigeon), Dove 62. e) Guinea Fowl f) Partridge	65. Lamb, Goat, Goat cheese, Sheep cheese 59. Crustaceans: Crab, Shrimp, Lobster, Crayfish	66. Pork 68. Rabbit 67. Venison: Moose, Deer, Cariboo
DRINKS	13. Dandelion coffee 13. Chicory coffee 14. Carob, Fenugreek tea 63. Cow milk 33. Pineapple juice 1b. Barley coffee 13. Chamomile	34. Papaya juice 35. Grape juice 12. Tomato juice 37. Mint Tea 9. Coffee	30. Wintergreen tea, Cranberry juice 64. Goat milk 32. Orange, lemon and grapefruit juice	27. Rosehip tea, Prune juice, Apricot juice 26. Apple juice, Pear juice 43. Green tea, Black tea 38. Ginger tea
VEGETABLES	56. Mushroom, Fungus 16. Zucchini, Cucumber 13. Lettuce, Dandelion, Artichoke 14. Alfalfa sprouts, Bean sprouts	12. Tomato, Eggplant, Peppers, Tomatillo 77. Dulse, Kelp 17. Asparagus, Onion, Chives, Leeks, Garlic 57. Nasturtium 75. New Zealand Spinach	18. Spinach, Chard, Lamb's quarters 73. Capers 19. Parsley, Celery, Fennel, Coriander	45. Okra 29. Olive 15. Cabbage, Radish, Cauliflower, Kale, Brussel Sprouts, Broccoli, Collard, Chinese Cabbage, Watercress, Mustard

STARCHY VEGETABLES

- 14. Dried Beans, Peas, Green Beans, Lentils, Soy Bean, Tofu, Jicama
- 25. Plantain
- 16. Squash, Pumpkin
- 13. Jerusalem Artichoke, Burdock
- 12. Potato
- 4. Corn
- 28. Avocado
- 70. Lotus Root
- 10. Taro, Malanga, Poi
- 20. Sweet Potato
- 15. Turnip
- 2. Bamboo Shoots
- 74. Yam

FRUIT

- 25. Banana
- 33. Pineapple
- 14. Tamarind, Carob pod
- 16. Honeydew Melon, Watermelon, Pumpkin, Cantaloup
- 48. Fig, Mulberry
- 54. Mango
- 34. Papaya
- 35. Grape, Raisins
- 24. Raspberry, Strawberry, Blackberry
- 23. Persimmon
- 7. Prickly Pear
- 40. Passion Fruit
- 41. Custard-Apple
- 42. Paw-paw
- 32. Orange, Lemon, Grapefruit, Tangerine, Lime
- 50. Date, Sago, Coconut
- 71. Litchi
- 30. Blueberry, Cranberry
- 21. Kiwi Fruit
- 26. Apple, Pear, Quince, Loquat, Rosehps
- 36. Guava
- 11. Rhubarb
- 27. Prune, Plum, Apricot, Cherry, Peach
- 31. Currant, Gooseberry
- 32. Pomegranate
- 78. Starfruit

FLOURS and GRAINS

- 56. Brewer's Yeast
- 1. Wheat, Bran
- 1a. Rye 1b. Barley
- 13. Psyllium
- 63. Gelatin
- 14. Chickpea, Soy, Lentil, Peanut, Carob flours
- 12. Potato Flour
- 4. Millet, Corn, Sorghum
- 77. Agar Agar
- 70. Lotus Root Flour
- 8. Tapioca, Yuca, Cassava Flour
- 3. Wild Rice
- 6. Rice, Rice Bran
- 18. Amaranth, Quinoa
- 11. Buckwheat
- 5. Oat, Oat Bran
- 9. Arrowroot

SEEDS and NUTS

- 14. Peanuts
- 52. Poppy Seeds
- 13. Sunflower Seeds
- 54. Cashew, Pistachio
- 16. Pumpkin seeds
- 53. Walnut, Pecan
- 44. Sesame Seeds
- 46. Flax Seeds
- 47. Filbert, Hazelnut
- 76. Pine Nuts
- 27. Almond
- 55. Chestnut
- 72. Macadamia Nuts
- 51. Brazil Nuts

SWEETS

- 41. & 57. Clover Honey
- 1b. Barley Malt
- 14. Carob Syrup
- 4. Molasses, Corn sugar - dextrose, glucose
- 50. Date Sugar
- 6. Rice Syrup
- 49. Maple Syrup
- 22. Pomegranate syrup (grenadine)

For explanation of numbers see page 3

Wheat Alternatives

Most people think that wheat and flour are synonymous terms. However there are many forms of flour derived from other grains, seeds, beans and vegetables that can be used in baking and cooking. Most of these are well known in various traditional cuisines and more recipes and ideas can be found in ethnic and international cookbooks.

Alternative flours seldom if ever work exactly like wheat. The high gluten content of wheat gives a wonderful texture and lightness to baked goods. Other flours with less or no gluten will give baked items that are heavier, more crumbly or more sticky but still quite edible and often delicious. Not all flours can be used in all situations. Some, such as tapioca and arrowroots, are good as thickeners. Just be careful not to over-cook them. Others such as potato and rice will add lightness to a recipe. Still others such as sweet (glutinous) rice flour, tapioca or arrowroot will help bind otherwise crumbly flours such as buckwheat and rice. If these flours are unavailable from the stores you are using, many of them can be made using a grain mill or your blender. For example, rolled oats or unroasted buckwheat blended into a powder and sieved will make good flours.

In addition to the flours, meals made from nuts or seeds can be made in a blender and used as toppings, pie crusts or to give extra flavour and nutrition to a baked item. They can be sprinkled on chopped fruit for a quick breakfast or used as a coating on broiled fish or poultry instead of bread crumbs.

If you are accustomed to eating sandwiches, substitute the bread with leafy vegetables such as lettuce or cabbage or with tortillas, rice wrappers or pancakes made with a different flour. Roll up the filling into the wrapper and munch away. Other vegetables such as celery sticks, avocado halves or green peppers can be stuffed with your favourite fillings. For breakfast spread nut-butters on sliced fruit or carrots.

If you have been eating bread with meals to fill up or to increase your carbohydrate intake use the starchy vegetables that you tolerate listed on the rotation diet page. Potatoes, sweet potatoes, turnips, carrots, squash, beans. . . . the list is endless and all can be cooked or steamed while the rest of your meal cooks. You could use rice cakes;

oat cakes, crisp baked or fresh tortillas or the muffins from the recipe section with your meal.

Noodles are available made from foods other than wheat. Rice, bean starch, pure buckwheat (careful; some are made with wheat), corn and sweet potato noodles are found in Chinese, Japanese or health food stores. Use them as described in the recipes or with your own pasta sauces.

When you bake with these flours you may find that flavours and textures are best when they are used in combinations such as buckwheat and arrowroot or millet and corn. Chick pea flour or light buckwheat flour often substitutes very well, in recipes using baking powder, for wheat flour. Do experiment with these flours. Don't be discouraged if a recipe fails initially. Write down your own experiments so that you do not lose a marvellous new discovery. You can use the list below of wheat flour equivalents to help guide your experiments.

If after meals you feel that you are still hungry and only bread will satisfy that hunger, you probably have a food addiction (see p. 4). Try eating more of a starchy vegetable with your meal. Be sure that you are eating enough protein by checking the table on page 42. You will find that if you continue to avoid wheat that you will lose that driving sense of hunger and dis-satisfaction.

These flours are available from health food stores, ethnic and specialty food stores. Prices can vary widely. As with any other food, flours are prone to spoilage when stored too long. Ask when they were milled. You could store them in your refrigerator or freezer. Avoid storage in damp or warm areas or in direct light.

Replace 1 cup wheat flour with:
Rye flour - 1¼ cups - not recommended with wheat allergy.
Barley flour - ½ cup - not recommended with wheat allergy.
Millet flour - 1 cup
Soy flour - 1⅓ cups - 20% of flour in recipe - bake at 25° lower than recipe.
Chick pea and other bean flours - ¾ cup
Rice flour - ¾ cup brown rice flour + ¼ sweet rice flour or ⅞ cup rice flour.
Oat flour - 1⅓ cups
Buckwheat flour - 1 cup

Tapioca flour - ½ cup - sauces, fruit fillings, glazes; do not boil or overcook.

Potato flour - ⅝ cup - combine with other flours for baking; good thickener.

Arrowroot flour - ½ cup - use as a thickener; do not overcook.

Corn flour - 1 cup - use as a thickener; do not overcook.

Amaranth flour - 1 cup

Cornstarch - ½ cup + rye, potato or rice flour ½ cup.

Quinoa flour - 1 cup

Cooked Grains

Grains can be served with any meal. They are great for breakfast, with nuts or seeds, or cooked or raw fruit. For lunch or dinner add some basil or oregano or other herbs and serve with beans, vegetables, poultry, fish or meat. You could also make a sauce or gravy from the recipes to go over them.

Puffed cereals, without sugar, such as millet, rice or corn are available at health food stores and occasionally super markets. With a milk-substitute, fruit puree or juice or home canned fruit they make a good breakfast. Buckwheat will be firmer if it is first pan-roasted particularly if you also mix in a beaten egg as it roasts.

When cooking grains it is best not to lift the lid too often while they cook. Add them to boiling water and turn the temperature down to a slow simmer. Depending on the specific variety of grain and how long it has been stored, you may need to slightly alter the recommended amounts of cooking water.

Beans

Beans are a good source of protein, especially in combination with grains. They are a good substitute for wheat and will add fibre to your meals.

Store beans in a tightly covered jar in a cool place.

Most dried beans should be presoaked to restore water lost in drying and to shorten cooking time. Use 6 cups of water for 1 lb. beans. Split peas and lentils do not need presoaking.

Freeze excess presoaked beans. Dry and place on cookie sheet in freezer. Freeze, then transfer to plastic bag.

If you forget to presoak them, place them in boiling water and boil for 2 minutes, then let stand, covered, for one hour. Cook in usual way.

To diminish 'gas' from eating: discard the soak water, cover with fresh water and cook for 30 minutes. Discard this water, add more fresh water and continue cooking. Be sure that the beans are well cooked before using.

How to Cook Grains and Cereals

Grain (1 cup dry)	Water	Cooking Time	Recipe on pages:
Brown rice	2–2½ cups	30–45 minutes	65
Buckwheat	1 cup	15–20 minutes	79, 102
Cornmeal	4 cups	20–30 minutes	56, 59
Millet	3½–4 cups	35–45 minutes	56, 59
Wild Rice	4 cups	40 minutes	70
Oats	2 cups	10–15 minutes	75
Quinoa	2 cups	15–20 minutes	68
Amaranth	2 cups	15–20 minutes	67

Puffed millet, rice, corn, etc., are available at health food stores for use as breakfast cereals.

Wheat-Free Diet
Foods to avoid:

Rye flour is often cross-reactive with wheat and is usually contaminated with some wheat flour.

Barley and malt are usually cross-reactive with wheat.

Beverages

Coffee substitutes and other beverages made from wheat, rye or barley products; Postum, Ovaltine etc. (Check labels for ingredients) Malted drinks, beer, ale, gin, whiskies, vodka.

Breads

Whole wheat, graham, gluten, gluten-free and white breads, rolls, muffins, and biscuits. Sweet rolls, johnny cake, pancakes, waffles, rusks, pretzels, bagels, zwieback, and crackers. Prepared mixes for the above. Rice, potato and soybean breads, rolls, muffins and biscuits; corn and rye breads, rolls, and muffins unless made without wheat flour.

Cereals

Wheat cereals and those containing wheat; cous-cous, triticale; cereal containing malt. (Read labels carefully)

Desserts

Cakes, doughnuts, dumplings and pastries, commercial sherbets, ice creams, ice cream cones, custards, cookies, pies, and puddings made with wheat products. Prepared mixes for cakes, cookies, ice creams, puddings and pie crusts, unless the list of ingredients shows no wheat products. Chocolate candy, candy bars and commercial candies that contain wheat. (Check labels)

Meats, Poultry, Game, Fish and Seafood

Swiss steak. Bread and cracker stuffings. Chili con carne, croquettes, fish, or meat patties and loaves, unless made at home without wheat products. (Commercial and dealer-prepared meats frequently contain wheat products, i.e. sausages, lunch meats, etc.) Breaded meats, fish or vegetables.

Miscellaneous

Malt products. Dumplings, noodles, spaghetti, macaroni, ravioli, vermicelli, soup rings, alphabets, etc. Starch - usually refers to wheat or corn. Hydrolized vegetable protein, MSG.

MINOR SOURCES:

Salad Dressings

Any salad dressing thickened with wheat flour.

Sauces and Gravies

Gravies, butter sauces, bouillon cubes, cream and white sauces unless homemade without wheat flour. Read labels on commercial sauces.

Soups

Cream unless made at home without wheat flour. Vegetable and meat soups, chowders and bisques if thickened with wheat products. (Read labels carefully)

*Wheat and Wheat products include: (1) all the following flours: white, bread, all-purpose, cake, pastry, self-rising, wheat, whole wheat, entire wheat, cracked wheat, graham, enriched, durum, phosphated; (2) also: wheat germ, bran, farina, semolina; (3) and in addition, cracker meal, bread crumbs and malt.

Note: When you buy packaged foods, read the labels carefully to be sure that the list of ingredients includes none of the above. When you purchase food lacking a list of ingredients and when you eat away from home, if in doubt about any food and accurate information cannot be secured, substitute a choice about which there can be no doubt.

Yeast, Malt and Mould-Free Diet
Foods to avoid:

Yeast Additives
The following foods contain yeast as an additive ingredient in preparation (often called leavening or baker's yeast):
1. Breads: light bread, hamburger buns, hotdog buns, rolls (homemade or canned), canned icebox biscuits, raised doughs, etc.
2. Pastries: cookies, crackers, pretzels, cakes and cake mixes, and so forth.
3. Meat: Fried in bread or cracker crumbs.

Yeast Forming
The following substances contain yeast or yeast-like substances, because of their nature or the nature of their manufacture or preparation (including brewer's and distiller's yeast and malt):
1. Vinegars (apple, pear, grape): These may appear as such or be used in these foods: ketchup, mayonnaise, French dressing, salad dressing, barbeque sauce, soya sauce, tomato sauce, sauerkraut, horseradish, pickles, olives, condiments, etc. (See Vinegar alternatives)
2. Fermented beverages: Whiskey, wine, brandy, gin, rum, vodka, beer, root beer, etc.
3. Fruit juices: citrus fruit (and others), either canned, frozen or boxed. Only home squeezed are mould free. Juices are probably a minor source.
4. Brewer's yeast, torula, engevita yeast, etc.

Yeast Derivatives
Certain vitamins contain yeast substances, therefore check the labels before taking them.

Malt Products
Cereals, candy and milk drinks that have been malted and some fermented beverages; also some bakery products.

Mould Foods
Mushrooms, truffles, morels, fungus.

Mould-containing Foods
1. Cheeses made with mould such as blue, gorgonzola, etc.
2. Foods which acquire mould growths during the preparation of processing or after exposure to air, even when refrigerated, such as ham, bacon, preserves, jams, jellies, syrups, canned fruit and vegetables, baked items, molasses, cheeses, dairy products.
3. Miso, tempeh, tamari, soya sauce.

All foods may develop surface mould after exposure to air. This is especially true of cheese (remove a thin surface layer before use) and ground meat (have it ground as you wait and cook it without delay). Leftovers should be covered, cooled quickly, frozen if possible and consumed quickly.

Vinegar Alternatives
1. Distilled white vinegar is made from corn and should be tolerated by yeast sensitive people.
2. Ask your pharmacist for 4–5% acetic acid. This is usually tolerated. It can be flavoured with sprigs of herbs like tarragon, thyme, rosemary, parsley, etc. About 3 Tbs. per quart and allow to steep 2 to 4 weeks.
3. Use lemon juice as your taste desires, on salads etc.
4. Ascorbic acid powder can be dissolved in water. It has an acid, lemon flavour.

Milk Alternatives

Nut and seed milks can be made quite simply in the blender. These milks can be used in any baking recipe that calls for dairy milk. They can also be used in place of dairy milk when cooking a hot cereal, e.g. oatmeal served with almond nut milk is quite tasty. Make up only as much as you need for one day.

Soy Milk

Available at all health food stores or mix soy milk powder with water. Experiment for thin or thicker milk. Available with or without added sugar. This is not suitable for babies who should be on breast or formula milk.

Cashew Nut Milk

1 cup raw cashews   2½ cups water
1 tsp. honey (optional)   ¼ tsp vanilla (Optional)

Blend dry nuts to form a meal. Gradually add water to form a milky consistency. Less water if a cream is desired. Also try using juice instead of water if sweeteners are being avoided.

Coconut Milk

1 cup hot water   ⅓ dessicated/shredded coconut

Blend. Strain if desired. If no blender is available, pour boiling water over coconut. Let stand ½ hour, squeeze out with a cheesecloth. Cool before use.

Almond, Hazelnut and Other Nut Milks

1 cup raw nuts   2½ cups water (less for cream)

Grind nuts in a blender until powdered. Gradually add water. Use or pour into recipe immediately before nuts settle or strain and use the residue elsewhere.

Sesame Milk

½ cup sesame seeds
2 cups water

1 Tbs. honey or maple syrup
  (optional)
2 cups water

Make same as nut milks. Also try with juice instead of water if sweeteners are being avoided.

Sunflower Seed Milk

Same as above. Less water for cream.

Soy Milk Custard

Use your favourite custard recipe - substituting soy milk (or any of the above milks) for cow's milk. Add a bit more vanilla.

Atole

Corn milk from Mexico. See page 62.

Milk-Free Diet
Foods to avoid:

Dairy Products
Milk, buttermilk, yogurt, kefir, ice cream, cheese*, butter, cream, sour cream, curd, whey, goat's milk, malted milk, dried, powdered or canned milks, whipping cream.

Baked Goods (all may contain milk)
Doughnuts, cakes, baking powder biscuits, breads, cookies, Zwiebac, waffles, hot cakes, piecrust, popovers, biscuits, muffins, pancakes, soda crackers.

Desserts and Sweets
Blanc mange, chocolate, pudding, junket, candy bars, nougat, custard, many candies, creme caramel, mousses.

Beverages
Cocoa drinks, malted milk, Ovaltine.

Soups
Cream soups, bisques, chowders.

Eggs
Scrambled eggs, souffles.

Meats and Vegetables
Creamed foods, foods prepared 'au gratin,' foods fried in butter, fritters, hamburgers, hash, hot dogs and other sausages (skim milk is used as a binder), weiner schnitzel, mashed potatoes, meat loaf, Bologna.

Sauces and Dressings
Cream sauces, gravies, hard sauces, some salad dressings (check labels), butter sauces.

Other

Popcorn with butter, rarebits, casein, caseinate, lactose. Non-dairy creamers may contain caseinate. Powdered artificial sweeteners may contain lactose. Margarine may contain milk solids.

* Although all cheeses are to be considered as milk products, a person not sensitive to milk may be found allergic to one or more cheeses. Therefore consider each kind and brand of cheese as a potentially specific allergen.

Dairy Product Alternatives:

Cheese

As a topping, instead of cheese, sprinkle foods with roasted and ground peanuts, almonds, pine nuts, pecans, sesame seeds or sunflower seeds.

To give more body to a recipe add sliced or crushed tofu.

In sandwiches, use nut butters or left over chicken or meats.

Ice Cream

See ice cream recipes on pages 54, 74, 106 and 107.

Yogurt

See Tofu Yogurt recipe on page 48.

Egg Alternatives

EGGS in most recipes can be replaced with one of these egg replacers. Choose the appropriate one depending on what role the egg plays in the recipe.

1. Commercial egg replacer usually contains potato starch, tapioca flour, and baking powder. Add more water to recipe when using it. Use for leavening or as a binder. Check labels, some may contain egg.
2. Tofu - ¼ cup for each egg. Good as a binder.
3. Gelatin - soften 1 tsp. of gelatin in 3 Tbs. boiling water. Stir until dissolved. Place in freezer. Take out when thickened and beat until frothy. Equals one egg. Use as a binder.
4. One tsp. baking powder for each egg substituted for leavening.
5. One tsp. vinegar (if tolerated) for each egg in a cake recipe - for leavening.
6. Cornstarch, arrowroot, tapioca and potato flour, slippery elm, soy flour, etc. act as thickening agents.
7. ⅓ cup soy flour and ⅔ cups water. Blend and heat in double boiler for 1 hour. Whip in 1 Tbs. oil and ¼ tsp. salt. Store in refrigerator. Use to bind cookies.
8. Boil 1 Tbs. Flaxseed in 1 cup water for 15 minutes. Add to muffins, etc. as a binder.
9. Combine 1 Tbs. psyllium seed husk with 3 Tbs. water and let sit briefly. Good binder.

Egg-Free Diet
Foods to avoid:

Beverages
Malted drinks, Ovaltine, egg nog, ovamalt, root beer, wine (many are cleared with egg white)

Baked Goods
Cakes, cake flour, cookies, doughnuts, macaroons, pastries, pancakes, waffles, pretzels, muffins, meringues, diet cookies, pie crust, French toast. Baking powder may contain egg (check the label). Glazed rolls, frostings, fritters, Bisquick.

Egg Products
Raw and cooked eggs, souffles, egg noodles, dried egg powder, omelets.

Sauces and Dressings
Mayonnaise, hollandaise, tartar sauce, boiled dressings, Caesar salad.

Meats and Vegetables
Patties, breaded foods, fritters, batters for frying, potato salad, sausages, meat loaf, packaged meats, hamburger, meat jellies, patties

Dessert and Candy
Puddings, marshmallow, chocolate, chocolate bars, custard, cream pies, ice cream, sherbet, soft candies, nougat

Soups
Noodle, consomme

Other names for Egg:
Albumin, conalbamin, globulin, livetin, mucoid, ovomucoid, ovalbumin, ovovitellin, vitellin and yolk. Commercial egg replacers may contain egg. Chicken eggs usually cross-react with eggs from other birds—avoid them too.

Corn-Free Diet
Foods to Avoid

Beverages
Beers, ales, lagers, hard liquors, wine, sparkling wine, except good imported wines and brandy. Soft drinks.

Corn Products
Corn flakes, flour, oil (mazola), starch, syrup, grits, hominy, corn chips, fresh, frozen, canned and popped corn; corn noodles, fritters, succotash, sugar, dextrose, glucose, invert sugar, sorbitol, mannitol, breakfast cereals.

Baked Goods
Corn breads, Indian pudding breads and pastries (check with baker), baking powder (check label), icings, frostings, pies, Bisquick, tortillas

Sauces and Dressings
White sauce, thickened sauce, white vinegar, acetic acid. Salad dressings, gravies, margarine, corn oil (mazola), deep fried foods.

Meats and Vegetables
Bacon, ham, processed cheese, pickles, sauerkraut, batters for frying, sausage, hot dog, luncheon meats, canned soups.

Desserts and Candy
Chocolates, caramels, coughdrops, hard candies, malted foods, ice cream, canned fruits, jelly, jam, preserves, custard, pudding.

Other
Tablets and capsules may contain corn starch. Adhesives. Laundry starch. Many products such as paper cups, plastic bags and container are dusted with corn starch to prevent sticking.

Soy Bean Free Diet
Foods to avoid

Beverages
Soy milk/drink, coffee substitutes (check label), protein drinks. Prosobee Isomil, Soyalac

Baked Goods
Some breads, rolls, cakes, pastries, and packaged mixes (check with baker). Roasted soy nuts are used to replace peanuts.

Cereals
Soy flakes, boxed breakfast cereals (check label), soy noodles.

Sauces, Dressings and Oils
Mayonnaise, salad dressings, 'vegetable' oils may contain soy oil, lecithin spread, miso, tamari, Crisco, Worchestershire etc., soy sauce, margarine.

Meats and Vegetables
Cold cuts, sausage, hot dogs, hamburger, hamburger extender, meat loaf. Ham and chicken if animals fed soy (only if exquisitely sensitive). Soy bean sprouts, tofu, bean curd, TVP (texturized vegetable protein), soy grits, vegetable protein, natto.

Desserts and Candy
Hard and nut candy, caramel, chocolate, ice cream, sherbert

Cheese
Processed cheese

Other names for soy
Lecithin, emulsifiers, TVP

Additive Free Diet

All packaged or processed food may contain additives which may or may not appear on the label or even be known to the manufacturer. The best way to avoid additives is to prepare all food from fresh ingredients.

Foods in Which Azo Dyes and Benzoates are often Added
Desserts and Treats

Candy
Caramels
Life Savers
Fruit Drops
Wintergreen Gums
Filled Chocolates
Soft Drinks
Ciders
Fruit Drinks
Ades (such as lemonade)
Jellies
Jams

Marmalades
Fruit
Gelatins
Stewed fruit sauces
Fruit yogurts
Ice cream
Pie fillings
Vanilla, butterscotch, and chocolate puddings
Caramel custard
Dessert sauces
Whips

Baked Goods

Bakery goods except plain rolls
Crackers
Cheese puffs
Potato chips

Cake and cookie mixes
Waffle and pancake mixes
Macaroni and spaghetti (certain brands)

Condiments and spreads

Cream cheeses
Low-calorie margarines
Mayonnaise
Salad dressing
Catsup (certain brands)

Mustard
Hollandaise
Mustard sauces
Sauces such as curry, fish, onion, tomato, white cream, bernaise

Other

Mashed rutabagas

Purees

Packaged soups and some
    canned soups

Canned or refrigerated preserves

Anchovies

Herring

Sardines

Fish balls

Caviar

Cleaned shellfish

Fish

Coloured toothpaste

Foods in Which Nitrates are often Added:

Dutch gouda or edam cheese

Pickles

Pork, canned meat, hot dog, bacon, salami, cold cuts

Foods in Which Sulphites are often added

Sulphites may be listed as potassium bisulphite, potassium meta bisulphite, potassium sulphite or sodium bisulphite, sodium meta bisulphite, sodium sulphite or sulphur dioxide.

Salads, especially salad bar items

Salad dressing (dry mix), relishes, dressing made with wine/cider
    vinegar

Avocado dip, guacamole

Pizza, pasta

Instant tea and coffee

Cake mixes, bread and roll mixes

Cookies, pie dough

Cod (dried), shellfish (fresh, frozen, canned or dried), shrimp, clams,
    lobster, scallops, crab

Canned and bottled fruit juices, including frozen

Fruit (cut-up fresh, dried or maraschino-type, purees, and fillings)

Vegetables (frozen, cut-up fresh, canned or dried)

Fresh mushrooms, canned mushrooms

Soups (canned or dried)

Sugar, corn syrup, pancake syrup, gelatin

Potatoes (cut-up fresh, frozen, dried or canned)

Sauces or gravies (canned or dried)
Sauerkraut, cole slaw, pickles
Snack foods
Beer, cider, colas, ginger ale, wine and wine coolers, Tang
Wine vinegar
Cheese spreads, Brie

It is important to note that some drugs also contain sulphites.

Additives in decaffinated coffee:
Methyline chloride or ethyl acetate

Additives in alcoholic beverages:
Agar-agar, clay, egg, seaweed, polyvinylpyrrolidine, casein, milk powder, citric acid, tannic acid, fumaric acid, potassium sorbate, bisulphites, captan and arsenic for filtering wine.
EDTA, glycerin, peptones, alginate, vitamin C, sulphites, flavours, colours, preservatives, MSG for beer and liquors.

Sugar Alternatives

Most people with food allergies find that they feel better if they avoid sugars and sweeteners. This may be due to an allergy to the sweetener or because of the metabolic effect of the sugar. Artificial sweeteners are also frequently not well tolerated by those with allergies. All concentrated and refined sugars have virtually the same metabolic effect on your body.

Honey and the other sweeteners listed do have some mineral and vitamin content but can be harmful to those who are sensitive to sugar. The sweeteners listed below will work well in place of sugar in some recipes but not in all. If you use a liquid sweetener you may need to reduce the amount of fluid or increase the flour in a recipe.

As an alternative for these sweeteners in recipes, use a fruit juice or fruit purée instead of the required water or milk alternative. You could add extra chopped fruit to a recipe to add sweetness.

In these and most recipes, the sweetener could be left out entirely. The recipe will not be as sweet but usually will otherwise work. If you do not wish to totally remove the sugar from a recipe, it can usually be cut down to a ¼ of that suggested in most cookbooks without harming the recipe.

Sweetener	Substitute for 1 cup sugar	Reduction of total liquid
Honey, Rice Syrup	¾ cup	⅛ cup
Maple Syrup, Molasses	¾ cup	⅛ cup
Date Sugar	1 cup	—
Fruit Juice	1 cup	—
Barley Malt	1 cup	⅓ cup
Date Jam (p. 65)	1½ cups	slightly
Raisin Pudding (p. 64)	¾ cup	⅛ cup
Prune Spread (p. 77)	¾ cup	⅛ cup

Exotic Ingredients

These items and others in the cookbook may be new to you. They are traditional items in some foreign cuisines. They are generally high in nutrients and may be delightful new taste experiences. Try them first using one of the recipes. Then make up your own variations. They can be found in oriental food stores, health food stores and some large supermarkets.

Agar Agar—is a seaweed that is an excellent replacement for gelatin. On cooking, it is clear, flavourless and quite stiff.

Amaranth/Quinoa—are seeds in the chenopod family originally from South America and are cooked like grains. They have a nut-like flavour and are very nutritious.

Carob—is a good chocolate substitute. It is naturally sweet with no caffeine content. It is derived from a pod of a middle-eastern tree. Available in powdered form it can be used instead of cocoa. Carob chips usually have been sweetened and contain other ingredients. The pods can be eaten whole. Watch for the very hard seeds.

Flaxseed—is useful as a source of dietary fibre and as a flour binder when cooked in water. Grind and sprinkle on cereals or fruits. Add to baked items. When ground, it goes rancid very quickly.

Glutinous/Sweet Rice—in flour form, this produces a very sticky dough. It is useful in making a drier flour like chickpea or rice flour more moist. It does not have sugar added.

Kelp, Dulse and Seaweeds—are available dry or powdered. many variations are available in natural food stores or Japanese groceries. They are a good source of iodine and minerals. Kelp or dulse can be used to replace salt or can be added to soups or sprinkled on vegetables.

Millet—is a grain popular in the Orient. It can be cooked into a soup-like consistency or with less water appears more like rice. It will take on flavours from spices or other foods or stocks. Because it turns rancid quickly after hulling, it should be kept refrigerated.

Slippery Elm Powder—is the powdered inner bark of an elm tree variety. It is useful in improving the texture of products such as the milk-free ice-cream recipes.

Tahini—is a butter made from sesame seeds with its own interesting flavour. Use it to replace peanut butter on muffins, etc., or pour over fruit, vegetables, grains or salads.

Taro, Malanga, Cassava, Jerusalem Artichoke, Yuca—are starchy, root vegetables available from some Chinese green grocers. They must be thoroughly cooked by boiling or baking before being used. Then treat them like potatoes. Cassava, from Africa, is toxic if not cooked well. Yuca is similar to cassava but does not contain the toxic chemical.

Tofu—is the curd of soybeans. It is not made with yeast. It is a good source of protein (see protein table) and can be prepared in many ways since it readily takes on the flavour of spices or other foods cooked with it. Natural food stores and Chinese groceries carry it.

Food Sources of Vitamins and Minerals

Foods generally have highest vitamin and mineral contents if eaten raw or minimally cooked with as little storage and exposure to heat and light as possible. They are best when allowed to fully ripen on the plant and grown in soils that have been organically fertilized. They are listed in order of the greatest concentration of the nutrient (i.e. if eaten in equal weights).

Calcium—kelp, cheese, dulse, carob, dark green leafy vegies, nuts, parsley, tofu, milk.

Copper—oyster, nuts, whole grains, dry peas, beef liver, peanuts, lamb, sunflower oil.

Chromium—brewer's yeast, calf's liver, beef, whole grains, oysters, potatoes.

Iodine—clams, shrimp, haddock, halibut, oysters, salmon, sardines, beef liver, pineapple.

Iron—kelp, brewer's yeast, pumpkin seeds, beef liver, sunflower seeds, millet, parsley, clams, nuts, dried prunes, beef, raisins, dark green leafy vegetables.

Magnesium—kelp, nuts, brewer's yeast, whole grains, tofu, green leafy vegies, soybeans.

Manganese—nuts, whole grains, dried peas, green leafy vegies, carrots, broccoli.

Molybdenum—lentils, beef liver, dry peas, cauliflower, green peas, brewer's yeast.

Nickel—canned foods, soy beans, beans, lentils, peas, nuts, whole grains, parsley.

Phosphorus—brewer's yeast, pumpkin and sunflower seeds, soy bean, cheese, nuts.

Potassium—seaweed, sunflower seeds, nuts, raisins, peanuts, dates, figs, avocado, yams, green leafy vegies, potatoes with skins, bananas, carrots.

Selenium—tuna, herring, smelt, Brazil nuts, shellfish, whole grains, liver.

Vanadium—buckwheat, parsley, unrefined vegetable oils, soybean, egg, oat, corn.

Zinc—oyster, beefsteak, lamb, nuts, dried peas, beef liver, milk, egg yolk, wholegrains.

Vitamin A—liver, egg yolk, dark green leafy vegies, deep yellow vegies, tomatoes, butter, whole milk, cheese.

Vitamin D—halibut liver oil, cod liver oil, fresh mackerel, sardines, herring, salmon, tuna, egg yolk, shrimp, liver, butter

Vitamin E—soy oil, corn oil, peanut oil, sweet potatoes, navy beans, brown rice, turnip greens, green peas, whole eggs, butter, oatmeal, liver.

Thiamine (B1)—sunflower seeds, pork, liver, yeast, lean meats, eggs, green leafy vegies, whole grains, berries, nuts, legumes.

Riboflavin (B2) = liver, milk, cheese meat, eggs, green leafy vegies, whole grains, legumes, sesame seeds.

Niacin (B3)—liver, meats, fish, sunflower seeds, whole grains, dry peas and beans, nuts, peanut butter.

Pyridoxine (B6)—brewer's yeast, sunflower seeds, wheat germ, calf liver, meats, whole grains, fish, soy beans, peanuts, yams, tuna, tomatoes, corn, carrots.

Biotin—liver, peanuts, egg yolk, nuts, cauliflower, mushrooms, dry peas, lima beans.

Pantothenic Acid—liver, dark green leafy vegies, asparagus, lima beans, kidney, nuts, whole grains, bran, meats, mushrooms, dry peas, soybeans, salmon.

Folic Acid—liver, dark green leafy vegies, asparagus, lima beans, kidney, nuts, whole grains, lentils.

Vitamin B12—clams, liver, kidney, beef, sole, scallops, haddock. Poor sources: milk, cheese, egg. No content—fruit, vegetables.

Vitamin C—citrus fruits, strawberries, cantaloupe, uncooked vegetables especially pepper, broccoli, cauliflower, kale, brussel sprouts, turnip greens, cabbage, tomatoes, potatoes. Especially sensitive to losses from heating, cutting of foods, and poor ripening.

Bioflavanoids—grapes, rosehips, prunes, citrus (especially white parts), cherry, plum, parsley.

Dietary Protein Requirements

Adequate dietary protein is essential for proper functioning of your body. You will not be able to regain or maintain your health if your protein intake is low. Particularly in vegetarian diets or when avoiding multiple foods it is important to be aware of your protein intake.

Age: 7—11 months	kgwt x 1.4 = ——— g.
1—3 years	22 g.
4—6 years	27 g.
7—9 years	33 g.
10—12 years	male: 41 g., female: 40 g.
13—15 years	male: 52 g., female: 43 g.
16—18 years	male: 54 g., female: 43 g.
19 + years	male: 56 g., female: 41 g.
pregnancy	add 20 g.
lactation	add 24 g.

If you do heavy work or have an infection, increase this amount by 25%. For example, a 30 year old male doing heavy work requires 56 grams x 1¼ = 70 grams of protein daily.

Vegetable protein has a lower biological activity, the body uses it less efficiently, so multiply the grams per day of vegetable protein by 0.73 before adding them to your animal protein total. For example if you eat 3½ oz. of tofu which has 8 grams of protein, 8 x 0.73 = 5.8 grams.

Dairy

Cottage cheese, 3½ oz.	17
Milk solids, 1 oz.	10
Milk, 1 cup.	9
Parmesan cheese, 1 oz.	10
Yogurt, 1 cup	8
Cheddar cheese, 1 oz.	7
Swiss cheese, 1 oz.	8

Nuts and Seeds

(28 g. or 1 oz. serving)

Pumpkin seeds	8
Sunflower seeds	7
Peanuts	8
Cashews	5
Sesame seeds	5
Walnuts	6
Brazil nuts	4

Meats and Poultry

(100 g. or 3½ oz. serving)

Turkey	31
Pork	29
Lean steak	25
Hamburger	25
Chicken	23
Lamb	20
Egg—one	6

Grains

(⅓ cup raw)

Wheat	8
Barley	6
Millet	6
Oatmeal	4
Rice	5
Bread, whole wheat, 1 slice	2.4

Seafood

(100 g. or 3½ oz. serving)

Canned tuna	24
Mackerel	22
Halibut	21
Salmon	20
Cod	18
Crab	17
Clams	14
Oysters	11
Scallops	15
Squid	16

Almonds	5
Hazelnuts/filberts	3
Chestnuts	1

Legumes

(1 cup cooked)

Soy	17
Mung beans	12
Peas	21
Black beans	12
Kidney beans	16
Garbanzo	13
Lima beans	10
Tofu, 3½ oz.	8
Lentils	12
Navy Beans	15
Soymilk	9

Vegetables

Potato, 1 medium	4
Soy sprouts, 1 cup	6
Green peas, 1 cup	7.5
Corn, 1 ear	4
Broccoli, 1 stalk	4
Cauliflower, 1 cup	3
Spinach, cooked 1 cup	3
Mung bean sprouts	4

Dietary Calcium Requirements

Sufficient calcium is essential for proper function of nerves, muscles and skeletal strength. Calcium intake has been found low in 60% of the population.

Age: 0—2 months	400 mg
2—6 months	500 mg
6—12 months	600 mg
1—2 years	700 mg
3—6 years	800 mg
6—8 years	900 mg
8—10 years	1000 mg
10—12 years	1200 mg
12—18 years	1400 mg
18 + years	1000 mg
pregnancy add	200 mg
breastfeeding add	1000 mg
post menopause add	500 mg

Vegetables (1 cup)		Parsley raw	122
Black beans dry	290	Spinach cooked	167
Chickpeas dry	300	Turnip cooked	54
Green beans	62	Torula yeast 1 oz.	120
Pinto beans	257		
Mary bean sprouts	20	**Fruit**	
Red kidney beans cooked	70	Raisin (⅔ cup)	49
Soy beans cooked	131	Apricot (10 halves)	16
Soy sprouts	50	Pear (10 halves)	59
Soy milk	55	Dates (10)	27
Beet greens cooked	144		
Broccoli cooked	136		
Chinese cabbage	52		
Carrots cooked	51		
Collards cooked	220		
Kale cooked	206		

Fish (3½ oz.)

Cod	29
Halibut	20
Herring	147
Oyster	85
Red Snapper	16
Salmon	175
Sardine (1 can)	303
Shrimp	63
Trout	45
Tuna, canned	9

Nuts

Almonds (12–15)	38
Brazil nuts (4)	28
Hazelnuts (10–12)	38
Peanuts, raw (1 oz.)	13
Sesame seeds (1 oz.)	35
Sunflower seeds (1 oz.)	34

Meats

Ground beef, lean ¼ lb.	14
Liver ¼ lb.	2
Chicken ¼ lb.	7
Lamb ¼ lb.	10
Egg—1	27

Dairy

Cheese (1 oz.):

Cheddar	200
Gouda	200
Mozzarella	163
Parmesan	329
Ricotta 1 cup	509
Milk 1 cup	291
Yogurt 1 cup	274

Yeast, Milk, and Wheat-free Breakfast
Day I

Salmon

Sliced smoked salmon or B.B.Q. tidbits can be eaten for breakfast or lunch. Eat alone or with the biscuits below. Great high protein meal.

Scrambled Tofu

Cut firm tofu into small pieces. Tofu can then be scrambled like egg (in an oiled skillet). Cook well. Add seasonings such as saffron, basil, curry.

Shakes or Smoothies

These tasty and filling drinks can be made by combining any nut or seed milk with fresh or frozen fruit in a blender. Let your imagination and allergies determine the combinations.

Banana Carob Milkshake

¼ cup cashew nuts (optional)
1 tsp. carob powder
1 drop vanilla (optional)

1 ripe banana
1 tsp. honey or carob syrup
  (optional)
1 cup soymilk or water

Blend 1 minute until smooth. Omit carob for plain banana milkshake.

Peanut Banana Shake

1 cup milk: soy, seed or nut
3 Tbs. carob powder
1 ripe banana

1–2 tsp. honey or carob syrup
  (optional)
¼ cup smooth peanut or cashew
  butter

Blend all ingredients

Carob Drink

4 cups milk: cashew, coconut, soy
1 Tbs. honey or maple syrup
  (optional)

½ tsp. vanilla
2 Tbs. oil
3 Tbs. Carob powder

Blend ingredients until smooth. Slowly add oil and blend together. Heat if desired. Do not boil.

Fruit and Nuts

Slice a banana or use pieces of pineapple or melon and serve with nut or seed milk. Sweeten with honey if desired.

Peanut Butter and Banana

Slice banana lengthwise and spread with peanut butter. Great!!

Chick Pea Muffins

2 cups chick pea flour
3 tsp. baking powder
1 Tbs. psyllium husk mixed with 3
  Tbs. water

¾ cup water or juice
¼ cup poppy seeds (optional)
¼ cup honey (optional)
3 Tbs. oil

Combine dry ingredients and add to wet. Bake at 350° F. for 20 minutes. Makes 10 muffins.

Peanut/Cashew Butter Cookies

1 cup peanut or cashew butter
¼ cup oil
¼ tsp. salt
½ tsp. baking powder

½ cup sweetener
½ tsp. vanilla (optional)
1½ cups chickpea flour
1 Tbs. psyllium husk soaked in 3
  Tbs. water

Preheat oven to 350°F. Mix liquid ingredients together until smooth. Add the flour. Mix well. Form into small balls with hands, place on oiled cookie sheet and flatten each with a fork. Bake about 10 minutes; be careful as they burn easily.

Chickpea Biscuits

1 cup chickpea flour
2 tsp. baking powder
½ Tbs. oil
1 Tbs. poppy seeds (optional)

¼ tsp. salt
1 Tbs. honey (optional)
¼ cup water or soy milk or juice

Mix dry ingredients. Stir oil and honey together and add to flour mixture. Add water to make a soft dough. Form dough into small balls and place on an oiled cookie sheet. Bake at 375°F. for 15–20 minutes. Best when warm.

Tofu Yogurt

Blend a cube of soft tofu into a smooth consistency. Mix with ½ tsp. vanilla, 2 Tbs. honey (optional) and ¼ tsp. ascorbic acid. Add fruit and mix gently.

Pumpkin Bread

¾ cup chickpea flour
¾ cup tapioca flour (skip over
tapioca on next rotation cycle)
¾ tsp. baking powder
¼ Tbs. cinnamon
¼ tsp. salt
¼ tsp. nutmeg
¼ tsp. cloves

¼ tsp. ginger
½ cup chopped figs
¼ cup butter or oil
¼ cup honey or sweetener
2 eggs or alternative
¾ tsp vanilla
1 cup pumpkin (cooked or pureed)

Combine dry ingredients together and mix well. Combine wet ingredients together and mix well. Gradually and gently blend wet and dry ingredients together. Spread in lined bread pan and bake at 350°F. for about 1 hour until a knife inserted in the middle comes out clean.

Poppy Banana Bread

1¾ cup chickpea flour
2¼ tsp. baking powder
¼ cup fig spread (see recipe)
¼ cup poppy or sunflower seeds
(optional)

1-1¼ cup banana pulp
¼ cup water
¼ cup oil
½ tsp. coriander

Cover 4 dry figs with water and soak or simmer the figs until they are quite soft. Blend into a smooth puree. Combine the dry ingredients and add to the creamed wet ingredients. Bake in a 8½ x 4½ inch pan at 350F for about 40 minutes.

Dandelion Coffee

1 tsp. ground, roasted dandelion
    root

1 cup water

Simmer or percolate for 10 minutes. Do not make too strong.

Chicory Coffee

1 Tsp. ground chicory root

2 cups water

Make as you would coffee with a filter or percolator.

Chickpea Waffle

1¼ chickpea flour
1 tsp. baking powder
¼ cup soft tofu (optional)

1½ Tbs. oil
¾ cup water

Mix the chickpea flour and baking powder. Blend together the tofu, oil and water. Stir into the flour and let sit for a couple of minutes. Pour half of the mixture into the heated waffle iron and cook till done. Makes two double waffles.

Lunch and Dinner
Day I

Roast Beef

Pre-heat oven to 550°. Trim off fat closely and place rib roast in oven. Turn down to 350° and cook 18–20 minutes per pound. One pound gives 3–4 servings. Use leftovers for other meals served on lettuce or chickpea biscuits.

Bean Pate

1 cup Romano or pinto beans
3 cups water
1 tsp. oil

1 tsp basil
1 tsp. cumin
½ tsp. pepper

Soak beans overnight if possible. Drain. Add to boiling water and cook until tender. Add more water if needed. Drain. Pass through grinder and mix in spices. Roll into lettuce leaves and serve with alfalfa sprouts and cucumber.

Bean Burger

2 cups cooked romano, soy, pinto or navy bean
2–3 Tbs. sesame butter (tahini)
½ tsp. cumin
Oil

½ cup chopped, sauteed and drained mushrooms (if tolerated)
¼ tsp. pepper
4 Tbs. chickpea flour

Mix all ingredients except flour. Shape into 2 inch balls. Flatten and dust with flour. Chill for 1 hour and sautée till brown in oil.

Salmon Salad

1. Use tinned or leftover salmon. Mix 7 oz. salmon thoroughly with 2 Tbs. oil and herbs (basil, oregano etc.) to taste.
2. Mix 7 oz. salmon with 2 Tbs. soy mayonnaise (see Gravies and Dressings) and serve on leaves of lettuce.

Lettuce Salad

Wash, tear and drain romaine or other leaf lettuce. Add flaked salmon, cucumber, alfalfa sprouts, lentil sprouts. Toss with 1 Tbs. oil per serving (see Gravies and Dressings for other dressings).

Baked Squash

Cut squash into halves. Bake face up at 375°F. for 1 hour, or until very soft. Add a little cinnamon or honey if desired. Serve with a salad.

Barley Muffins

2 cups barley flour (if tolerated)
½ tsp. salt
2 cups milk (peanut, cashew or soy)
  or water or juice
¼ cup oil

2 tsp. baking powder
½ cup honey or carob syrup
(optional)
¼ tsp. vanilla

Mix wet ingredients with wet, dry ingredients with dry. Add wet to dry mixture and stir lightly. Lumps are alright. Add presoaked pieces of figs or pineapple chunks if desired. Serve with peanut or cashew butter. Bake at 350°F. for 20 minutes.

Sprout Salad

Toss bean sprouts, sprouted lentils and alfalfa, endive or escarole with soy oil.

Zucchini

Slice a washed zucchini into ½ inch chunks or ¼ inch slices. Lightly fry zucchini chunks in sunflower oil with sweet basil or oregano.

Lentil Nut Loaf or Patties

3 cups lentils (medium soft puree)
½ cup ground pumpkin seeds
1 Tbs. soy sauce or ½ tsp. salt
basil and sage

4 Tbs. oil
1½ cups raw nuts (chopped
peanuts, cashews)
½ cup chickpeas, cooked or canned

Mix well. Bake in oiled loaf pan for 1 hour at 350°F. Good with peanut or cashew gravy. Or form into hamburger size patties and bake for 20 to 30 minutes.

Chickpea Crepe

1 cup chickpea flour
½ cup water or more if needed

¼ tsp. salt
¼ cup tofu (optional)

Blend until smooth. Pour on hot, well oiled griddle. Cook 2 minutes then flip. Cook 30 seconds or until golden.
—stuff with fresh fruit for breakfast, e.g. bananas or pineapple
—cooked beans, beef, fish, etc. for lunch or dinner
If not rotating, use a 50% mixture of chickpea and buckwheat flours.

Jerusalem Artichokes

Delicious—steam or boil until soft—slice and add a nut gravy. Tastes like a flavourful potato.

Herbed Chick Peas

Saute 1 cup cooked or canned (drained) chickpeas in 2 Tbs. oil. Sprinkle lightly with basil, oregano or rosemary.

Chick Pea Salad

To 1 cup cooked or canned chickpeas add 7 oz. of canned artichoke hearts. Add dressing or oil and ¼ tsp. paprika, ¼ tsp. basil, ¼ tsp. oregano to chickpeas.

Curried Lentils

1 cup lentils
2 cups water

1 tsp. curry powder
1 Tbs. oil

Cook lentils in water until tender. Heat oil in a skillet. Add curry powder. Heat briefly and add cooked lentils. Mix and simmer 5 minutes.

Pizza Crust

1 cup chickpea flour
½ cup sweet rice flour (skip rice on next rotation cycle)

2 tsp. baking powder
2 Tbs. oil
water as needed—about ½ cup

Sift flours and baking powder together. Add oil and water. Spread out on an oiled cookie sheet. Add toppings and bake at 450°F. until it starts to brown, about 20–30 minutes. Produces a thin crust.

Papadums

These are thin and crisp like large potato chips made from lentil flour and are available in East Indian food stores. They should be heated carefully in an oven and will become crisp like a chip.

Mie Goreng—Indonesian Noodles

¼ lb. bean starch/bean thread noodles
4 cups boiling water
½ cup chopped peanuts or cashews
2 Tbs. oil

¼ tsp. salt (optional
2–3 slices ginger root
1 cup snow peas or peas
1 cup zucchini, sliced thinly

Boil noodles briefly, about 5 minutes, until "al dente" and drain. Carefully roast nuts in a pan for 3–5 minutes or use roasted nuts. Sauté ginger and vegetables until soft and add to noodles with nuts. Add salt or 2 Tbs. soy sauce (wheat free), if not yeast sensitive. You can use leftover or sautéed beef instead of nuts. Sauté for 3 more minutes and serve hot. Serves 2.

These noodles become translucent when cooked.

Dessert
Day I

Fruit Ice Cream

1½ cups pineapple juice
1 tsp. slippery elm powder (from
   health food store)
juice of ½ lemon or more pineapple
   juice

¼ cup honey (to taste—optional)
1 cup cashews
2 Tbs. oil

Blend above ingredients until smooth. Add chopped up fruit—either 1 cup figs (soaked), mango, banana or pineapple—whatever the diet allows (optional). Pour into flat pan and freeze. Serve before it gets too hard. Children love this.

Vanilla Ice Cream

Soak: 1 Tbs. agar flakes (from health food store)
1 cup water
Boil one minute. Cool one minute.
Add: 1 cup cashew nuts
¼ cup honey
1 Tbs. vanilla
2 cups water
⅓ cup oil (soy)—optional
Blend above ingredients except oil. Add oil slowly while blending. Blend again. Freeze in bowl or flat dish.

Frozen Banana

Frozen banana is delicious. Peel, cut into chunks and freeze. Pour on 1–2 Tbs. of pineapple, lemon or lime juice (optional) and serve. Alternatively, blend the semi-frozen chunks and serve, or re-freeze for later use.

Fried Banana

Peel a not overly ripe banana. Slice in half lengthwise. Fry in 4 Tbs. oil. Serve with 1–2 Tbs. of pineapple, lemon or lime juice (optional). It will become very soft and sweet.

Carob Chip Cookies

½ cup sweetener   2 eggs or egg replacer
½ cup oil   1 tsp. vanilla

Combine the above in a bowl and add:

½ cup soy flour   2 tsp. baking powder
¾ cup chick pea flour   ½–1 cup carob chips

Form into 1½ inch flat cookies. Bake at 375°F. for 8–10 minutes.

Banana Cookies

4 figs   1 medium banana
1 cup chick pea flour   ¼ cup oil
1 tsp. baking powder

Soak the figs in boiling water and leave overnight. Combine the chick pea flour and baking powder. Blend the soaked figs, banana and oil until smooth. Add to the flour and mix thoroughly. Spoon onto a greased cookie sheet. Press down with a wet fork and bake at 350 for 15 minutes.

Yeast, Milk, Wheat-Free Breakfast Day II

Millet Cereal

3½–4 cups water   *1 cup millet*

Wash millet thoroughly. Bring water to a boil, add millet (soak overnight to hasten cooking if desired), then simmer gently for 30 minutes. Sweeten with maple syrup and fresh fruit. Add a non-dairy milk if desired to increase flavour and protein count or add dry roasted nuts.

Millet Raisin Pudding

¾ cup millet   *2 Tbs. corn syrup (optional)*
¼ tsp. salt   *1 tsp. vanilla*
4 cups water or juice   *½ cup sesame seeds or walnut pieces*
½ cup raisins

Cook washed millet in water and salt until it boils. Add remaining ingredients and pour into a casserole dish. Cover and bake at 350°F. for 1 hour. Stir occasionally. Good served with berries. Can be flavoured with a pinch of cinnamon, ginger, cloves or cardamon. If you are not rotating, try with chopped dates and slices of raw apple—in place of raisins.

Cornmeal (Polenta)

½ cup cornmeal   *2 cups water*

Add cornmeal to water and bring to boil while stirring. Cook 15 minutes or longer. Lower heat and stir frequently until the cornmeal has thickened. If too thick add more water. You may want to add ¼ tsp. salt plus fruit or vanilla.

Potato Pancakes

3 large potatoes
3 eggs (optional if flour used)

1 tsp. oats, barley, rice, buckwheat, millet or potato or corn flour (optional)
1 large onion (optional)

Grate potatoes coarsely. Grate onion finely. Add to potatoes and mix with eggs and flour. Add oil to hot skillet. Ladle spoonfuls of batter onto the hot skillet. Fry quickly until brown and turn. Drain on paper.

Tortillas

1 cup Masa harina   ½ cup warm water

Work water into the masa to make a soft dough. Shape into a ball, cover and let sit for 20 minutes. Divide into 6 balls. Line a tortilla press with plastic and press each or use a heavy skillet to make a thin flat tortilla. If necessary, add a little masa or water if too sticky or crumbly. Cook on a preheated skillet until lightly spotted with brown. Turn once.

Alternatively, you can buy frozen tortillas and lightly bake or fry them.

Tacos

Frozen or packaged tortillas or taco shells can be lightly baked or fried. Roll up with avocado, tomato, onion, green pepper, chicken, egg slices or whatever else you fancy.

Cod or Carp

Both are available smoked and make a good, quick breakfast or lunch.

Fruit and Nuts

Slice papaya and add berries or grapes and top with walnuts or sesame seed milk (see milk alternatives).

Lunch and Dinner
Day II

Fish in Tomato Sauce

1 small onion
1 clove garlic chopped
¼ tsp. sage
¼ tsp. kelp

2 Tbs. oil
1 chili pepper or dash of cayenne
¼ tsp. thyme
¼ tsp. marjoram
32 oz. can of tomatoes or 4–5 fresh
    peeled tomatoes
1½ lbs. of fish–cod, haddock, etc.

Sauté one chopped small onion in 2 Tbs. oil. Add spices and herbs. Add 32 oz. tin of tomatoes (or 4 fresh) puréed or chopped fine. Simmer for ½ hour.

Cut fish into 2 inch pieces and add to sauce. Simmer for 10 minutes. Serve over millet—see page 56, or over polenta–see page 56.

Macaroni with Quick Tomato Sauce

1½ cup corn macaroni
6 cups boiling water
1 large can plum tomatoes or 5 large
    ripe tomatoes
2 Tbs. oil

⅛ tsp. cayenne (optional)
6 oz. tomato paste
½ onion, finely chopped
½ green pepper, finely chopped
¼ tsp. kelp, dulse or salt (optional)

Blend or strain the tomatoes. Sauté other vegetables and add to tomatoes. Bring to boil and simmer about 10 minutes. (Boil macaroni until softened. Do not overcook; it should be springy, not mushy.) Pour sauce over noodles. Serves two. If you like, add ½ chopped chicken to the sautéing vegetables. Spice up the sauce with any herbs you like such as oregano and basil.

Sesame Scalloped Potatoes

Chopped onions
1 tsp. basil
sliced potatoes

½ chopped green or red pepper
1 Tbs. parsley
1 quart sesame milk (page 27)

Slice scrubbed potatoes into casserole dish until half full. Add a layer of chopped onions and ½ chopped green pepper. Add 1 tsp. basil and 1 Tbs. chopped parsley. Complete filling casserole with sliced potatoes and add enough unstrained sesame milk to cover, approximately 1 quart. Bake at 425°F. for 1 hour or until soft.

Quick Millet Loaf

1 cup raw millet
1 cup tomatoes
1 medium onion, cut into pieces
½ cup walnuts or pecans (optional)
1 tsp. Italian seasoning

2 cups water
1 tsp. salt
1 can black olives, quartered
(2 finely chopped dried tomatoes)
    optional

Put millet into casserole. Blend together tomatoes, onion, nuts and water. Add blender ingredients and remaining ingredients to millet. Mix. Bake at 325°F. for 2 hours. If too dry add more water. Millet can be cooked in advance in which case bake only 25 minutes.

Cornmeal/Polenta

2 cups cornmeal

8 cups water

Add cornmeal to water and bring to boil while stirring. Cook about 30 minutes stirring frequently and pour into an oiled 8 x 14" pan. Top with fish in tomato sauce (see p. 17), spicy sauteed vegetables or any other topping. If not rotating try beans or meat sauce.

Potato/Taro Chips

Slice raw potatoes or taro as thinly as possible. Place on lightly oiled tray. Broil for about 15 minutes. Turn and broil on other side. Watch to prevent burning. Sprinkle with basil or other herbs, before broiling, if desired.

Corn Chips

Slice frozen (thawed) or fresh, soft corn tortillas into 6–8 wedges. Bake at 350°F. till crisp. These are low-fat, low-salt crispy corn chips.

French Corn Cakes

2 cups corn kernels (fresh, frozen or canned)
3 eggs
2 Tbs. oil
⅓ cup corn flour
dash of salt

Cook fresh or frozen corn. Drain canned corn. Puree all ingredients in a blender. Heat a large heavy frying pan. Add oil and pour out small 2½ inch rounds of batter. Press down lightly with a fork. Cook until starting to brown, flip and cook the other side.

Corn Tamales

4 cups canned, fresh or frozen corn kernels
¾ cup chopped onions (optional)
1 cup chopped tomatoes
dash salt
½ tsp. chili powder
2 Tbs. chopped scallions or green pepper
2 Tbs. oil

Drain canned corn. Mix all ingredients together. Cut out 12 six inch aluminum foil squares. Place part of the mixture in the centre of each square. Roll up foil and twist the ends to seal it securely. Cook in boiling water for 45 minutes. Drain and serve. Serves six.

Taro

Peel off the thick brown skin. The white flesh will turn red if exposed to air. Cut into small pieces and cook as you would a potato, however it will take longer to cook. It is good in a vegetable or meat stew.

Ratatouille (Vegetable Stew)

1 onion, chopped
2 cloves garlic, chopped
¼ cup parsley or chives, chopped
1 eggplant, cut in 2″ cubes
1–2 green peppers, cut in chunks
1 tsp basil

pinch of salt
2–3 leeks, slices—greens included
¼ cup olive oil
pinch of red or black pepper
2 Tbs. tomato paste mixed in ½ cup
    water
3 ripe tomatoes, chopped

Saute onion and garlic in oil. Add the rest of the ingredients. Put on a tight fitting lid and cook on low to medium heat for ½ hour. Vegetables cook in their own juice so don't lift the lid too often.

Corn Bread

⅛ cup corn syrup
1 cup milk alternative
5 Tbs. oil
1 egg or 2 Tbs. flaxseed egg replacer
    (page 30)

1 cup cornmeal
1 cup cornflour
3 tsp. baking powder
½ tsp. salt

Combine oil, corn syrup and liquid. Beat in egg. Mix dry ingredients and add to liquid mixture. Combine and bake at 350°F. for about 20 minutes. Best baked in a pie plate or a small loaf tin.

Chicken/Avocado Tostada

Bake or fry tortillas until crisp. Apply a thin layer of mayonnaise. Top with generous layers of chicken and/or avocado, tomato, green onions, green peppers. Top with hot chile pieces or hot chile sauce.

Guacamole

1 cup mashed avocado
⅓ cup chopped tomato (optional)
1 Tbs. chopped onion (optional)
1 garlic clove, crushed (optional)

1 tsp. water with ¼ tsp. ascorbic
    acid
2 tsp. chopped parsley
chopped hot peppers or cayenne
    pepper to taste

Blend all ingredients together to a fine consistency. Serve with corn chips. (See recipe p. 60)

Atole

This pre-Columbian Mexican beverage is still regularly served. It is best when served hot off the stove. Great on cool, wet days, If you are sensitive to sugar, this is not for you.

3 cups water

1 stick cinnamon

2 Tbs. corn syrup

½ cup masa harina or corn flour

¼ cup water

Bring 3 cups of water and the cinnamon stick to a boil. Remove from heat and let stand for 1 hour. Remove cinnamon stick. Mix corn flour into ¼ cup water until smooth. Slowly add to cinnamon water. Stir in the corn syrup and stir over medium heat until the atole starts to thicken. If too thick, add more water. Makes 3 servings. It can be varied by flavouring with pureed fruits rather than cinnamon.

Greek Salad

1 tomato

1 green or red pepper

½ spanish onion

small bunch New Zealand spinach (if available)

Slice the tomato into small wedges and the pepper into ½ squares. Slice the onion thinly and separate the sections. Toss with New Zealand spinach and dress with oil and vinegar. Walnut oil has a wonderful flavour. Use oregano or basil vinegar if you have made it in advance.

Basil Vinegar

2 cups distilled white vinegar

2 Tbs. fresh sweet basil or

2 tsp. dried basil

Crush fresh herbs slightly and add to vinegar. Cover and let sit for one or two weeks. If too strong add more vinegar.

Crush dried herbs into vinegar. This can be used after one hour.

Dessert
Day II

Berry Agar Mould

2 Tbs. agar-agar flakes
1 cup cold water
1 cup hot water

1 cup berry juice
¼ cup corn syrup or sweetener

Mix agar-agar flakes with cold water and let sit for 1 minute. Add hot water. Boil 2 minutes, let cool and add juice and sweetener. Cover bottom of glass mould with berries. Pour part of jelly over fruit and allow to set. Repeat process to form layers of fruit and jelly.

Strawberry Crisp

Filling:
4 cups fresh sliced strawberries
2 Tbs. cornstarch

¼ cup corn syrup (to taste, optional)

Simmer strawberries until cooked. Add cornstach and syrup and simmer until it begins to thicken. Place in bowl and cover with topping of ground walnuts, pecans and sesame seeds or make a lower crust of ground nuts, and seeds with a little oil and add strawberry filling. Bake in oven at 350° for 15 minutes.

Berry Pudding

¾ cup berry or grape juice
1 Tbs. corn starch
1 Tbs. potato flour

3 egg yolks (optional)
2 cups sliced and mashed berries

Combine juice, cornstarch, and potato flour in a pan. Cook for 10 minutes over medium heat. Stir occasionally until thickened. Reduce to low heat and add egg yolks. Cook 5 minutes until thick and smooth. Remove from heat and stir in berries.

Raisin Pudding

1 cup raisins   *1 cup hot water*
⅓ cup walnuts or pecans (optional)

Wash raisins thoroughly. Soak in hot water until softened. Blend raisins, nuts, and water until smooth. Very sweet. Good as is or use as topping on cereals or as a sugar alternative in recipes.

Puffed Millet Squares

½ cup sesame butter (tahini)   *3 Tbs. oil*
½ cup raisin pudding (see above) *3 cup puffed millet*

In a blender combine sesame butter, raisin pudding and oil. Blend until smooth. Stir into puffed millet until well combined. Chill and serve.

Fresh Strawberry Pie

¼ cup water   *4 cups strawberries*
2 Tbs. corn starch

Line a 9 inch pie plate with a crust from the list below. Mix the corn starch with water until the paste is smooth. Clean and slice the strawberries. Pour the corn starch mixture over the berries, gently stir and allow to sit for 15 minutes. Pour berries into pie crust. Line pie plate with Cooked Millet Crust below. Bake at 450 for ten minutes and then at 350 for 40 minutes.

Cooked Millet Crust

½ cup millet   *½ cup water*

Cook millet until water is absorbed. It should be slightly sticky. If not add a little more water and cook longer. Pour into pie plate and press into thin layer. When adding fruit to this be sure that it covers the edges of the crust. The crust will dry out where it is exposed. If you like add ½ cup ground sesame seeds to the millet.

Yeast, Milk, Wheat-Free Breakfast Day III

Brown Rice Pudding

2 cups cooked brown rice
¼ cup chopped dates

1½ cups hazelnut milk (see page 26)

Mix all ingredients. Pour into deep casserole dish. Bake 20 minutes at 325°F. Serve hot with additional nut milk.

Rice Cakes

Purchase at health food stores.
Serve with butter made from tolerated nuts.

Citrus Fruit Salad

Separate sections of oranges, grapefruit, tangerine.
Serve with coconut milk. Top with coconut or ground hazelnuts or sunflower seeds.

Red Snapper

Bake, broil or poach. Bake covered for 10 minutes per 1 inch thickness or until flakey.

Date Jam

2½ cups chopped dates
2 tsp. (organic) orange or lemon rind

1½ cups hot water

Soak dates in hot water until soft. Blend everything. To make smoother cook at low heat stirring constantly and adding more water if necessary.

Date Nut Jam

Add 1 cup of finely chopped filberts or hazelnuts to above recipe.

Non-Dairy Tapioca Pudding

2 cups nut or seed milk
4 Tbs. tapioca

maple syrup to taste (optional)
1/4 tsp. vanilla (optional)

Soak tapioca in nut or seed milk for 15 minutes. Heat to boiling point. Stir occasionally until mixture begins to thicken. Do not allow to burn. Cool. Add sliced fruit and coconut and serve warm.

Fruit Juice Tapioca Pudding

The same as Non-Dairy Tapioca Pudding above using fruit juice such as orange or grapefruit instead of nut or seed milk.

Rice Filbert Muffins

3/4 cup rice
1/4 cup sweet rice flour
2 Tbs. rice syrup or date sugar
  (optional)
3/4 cup water or juice

3 tsp. ground filberts
1 Tbs. oil
2 tsp. baking powder
1 cup frozen or fresh blueberries or
  chopped dates (optional)

Mix oil, water and rice syrup together. Add to dry ingredients. Bake at 400°F. for 20 minutes. Makes 6.

Fluffy Rice Pancakes

1 1/4 cup brown rice flour
1/2 cup tapioca flour
1/4 cup sweet rice flour

2 cups water or nut milk or juice
1 tsp. baking powder
2 Tbs. oil

Sift together dry ingredients. Add blueberries if desired. Mix liquid ingredients and add to dry. Cook until lightly golden.

Tapioca Pancake

1 cup hazelnut flour (make in
   blender from whole nuts)
½ cup tapioca flour
2 tsp. baking powder

1 cup water or juice
1½ Tbs. oil
2 Tbs. rice syrup or date sugar
   (optional)

In a blender mix all ingredients well. Pour into a hot, oiled skillet and cook until done.

Tapioca Crepe

1 cup hazelnut flour (make in
   blender from whole nuts)
½ cup tapioca flour
2 tsp. baking powder

1 cup water or juice
1½ Tbs. oil
2 Tbs. rice syrup or date sugar
   (optional)

In a blender mix all ingredients well. Pour into a well-oiled, preheated skillet over medium heat, to thinly cover bottom. Cook 2 minutes or until top starts to dry. Turn and cook 30 seconds. Crepes are chewey, not fluffy. If not rotating, 2 Tbs. soft tofu can be added for lightness.

Carrot Bread

1 cup rice flour
½ cup tapioca flour
or 1¼ cup amaranth flour instead of
   rice and tapioca
2 tsp. baking powder
¼ tsp. cinnamon
¼ tsp. salt
¼ tsp. nutmeg

¼ tsp. cloves
1 tsp. ginger
½ cup date jam
¼ cup oil
1 cup nut milk or carrot or orange
   juice
¾ cup grated carrots
¾ tsp. vanilla

Combine dry ingredients together and mix well. Combine wet ingredients together and mix well. Gradually and gently blend wet and dry ingredients together. Batter will be very thick. Spread in lined pans and bake at 350°F. for about 1 hour until a knife inserted in the middle comes out clean.

Amaranth Cereal

1 cup amaranth   *2 cups cold water*

Combine in a saucepan. Cover and bring to a boil. Reduce heat and simmer for 25 minutes. Serve with fruit and nuts. Serves 3. For one serving use ¼ cup amaranth and 1 cup water. Use amaranth to replace millet in any recipe.

Herring, Sardine

Pickled herring (if not yeast sensitive) or canned sardines with rice cakes make a quick breakfast or lunch.

Quinoa Cereal

1 cup quinoa   *2 cups water*

Rinse well under running water. Bring water to boil. When rapidly boiling add quinoa. Reduce heat and let simmer until all water absorbed. Use quinoa to replace millet in any recipe. Serves 3 people.

Rice Waffle

1 cup brown rice flour   *1 Tbs. oil*
1 Tbs. sweet rice flour   *¼ cup date jam (see page 65)*
1 tsp. baking powder   *1⅞ cups water*

Mix flours and baking powder. Blend together oil, date jam and most of the water. Add to flour mixture. Add rest of water to make slightly thick batter. It will thicken as it stands. Pour half into pre-heated and well oiled waffle iron. Do not make the waffle too thick or it will not cook completely. Makes two double waffles.

Lunch and Dinner
Day III

Shrimp and Spinach Salad

Wash, drain, and tear spinach. Wash shelled shrimp, drain and add to spinach. Top with pine nuts and oil and lemon juice dressing (see Dressing and Gravies). Use 1 Tbs. per serving.

Carrot and Celery Juice

Juice 1 stick of celery and 5–6 carrots. Delicious and filling.

Beet Salad

Steam beets until soft. Peel and slice into ¼ inch wide pieces, let cool and add a lemon and oil dressing (¼ cup oil and 3 Tbs. lemon juice).

Carrot Salad

1. Slice thinly and steam until soft. Toss with oil and lemon juice dressing. (See Gravies and Dressings.) Use dill instead of mustard.
2. Grate coarsely. Add orange juice and orange or tangerine segments or add coconut with a lemon and oil dressing.

Rice Crackers

Top with hazelnut butter, shrimp pate or goat's milk cheese.

Carrots Vichy

Place in saucepan:
2 cups scraped, sliced carrots
½ cup boiling water
1 Tbs. sweetener (optional)

1 Tbs. oil
1 Tbs. lemon juice

Cover the pan tightly. Cook over quick heat until water evap Let brown in the oil. Serve sprinkled with chives or parsley

Lamb

Broil lamb chops 4 inches from heat on both sides till done, or use minced lamb to make lamb patties as you would with beef. Serve with rice crackers and steamed carrots.

Beet and Swiss Chard Salad

Cook Beets. Peel, slice thinly. Add cooked, drained, chopped swiss chard or spinach. Toss with oil that has been warmed in small pan with sliced garlic clove. Do not overheat oil. Add lemon juice if desired.

Fish

Poach, bake or broil, snapper, blue fish or yellow perch. Bake covered for 10 minutes per each inch of thickness or until flaky.

Wild Rice Ring

1 cup wild rice	¼ cup oil
4 cups boiling water	½ tsp. basil or parsley

Wash the rice and cook it without stirring until tender. Add the herbs and oil. Place the rice in an oiled 7″ ring mould. Place in a pan of hot water and bake at 350°F. for 20 minutes. Carefully empty the ring onto a platter. You can fill the centre with shrimp or lamb.

Parsnips

Peel, then cut in half 4 medium sized parsnips. Place in oiled, oven-proof dish. Oil parsnips with 2 Tbs. oil. Sprinkle with ¼ tsp. salt. Add to dish ¾ cup stock or water. Cover and bake until tender, approximately 45 minutes. Or prepare as for Carrots Vichy.

Carrot Soup

½ lb. carrots, sliced thinly
1 onion, sliced thinly (optional)
2 Tbs. oil
½ cup cooked brown rice
4 cups vegetable stock or water, or 2
    cups either stock or water and 2
    cups nut or seed milk.

½ tsp. dried thyme
½ tsp. kelp
pinch of paprika, nutmeg, cinnamon

Add oil to heavy saucepan and heat. Add carrots and onion. Cover and steam 5 minutes. Add stock, rice and seasonings. Cover and simmer for 20 minutes. Put in blender (2 batches). Return to saucepan and heat.

Rice Wrappers

These thin flexible wrappers are available from Chinese or Vietnamese grocers. Wrap them around vegetables or stuff with your favourite sandwich filling. Use instead of wheat or corn tortillas. To prepare briefly dip the dry wrapper in cold water and handle carefully.

Mie Goreng (Indonesian Noodles)

¼ lb. rice noodles
4 cups boiling water
½ cup filberts, chopped
2 Tbs. oil
¼ tsp. salt (optional)

2–4 slices ginger root, chopped
1 cup coarsely grated carrots
1 cup celery, sliced thinly
1 cup chopped spinach

Boil noodles in water until 'al dente,' and drain. Carefully roast nuts in pan for 3–5 minutes or use roasted nuts. Sauté ginger and vegetables until soft and add to noodles with nuts. Add salt. You can use leftover or sautéed carrot or shrimp instead of nuts. Sauté for 3 more minutes and serve hot. Serves 2, or 1 very hungry person.

    These noodles can alternatively be served with your favourite pesto sauce.

Amaranth Muffins

1¾ cups amaranth flour or 1¼ cups amaranth and ½ cup filbert flour (make in blender)
¼ cup tapioca flour
1 tsp. cinnamon

½ tsp. vanilla (optional)
¼ cup oil
¾ cup water or juice
2–4 Tbs. date sugar or date jam (page 65) (optional)

Combine dry ingredients. Mix liquid ingredients and add to dry. Bake at 375°F. for 20 minutes. If you like, add 1 cup chopped dates or 1 cup blueberries or cranberries and/or ¼ cup chopped filberts to batter. Makes 8–10.

Millet Primavera

6½ cups chicken stock
2 cups millet
½-1 cup cubed chicken (optional)
2¼ cups in total of chopped red and green peppers, asparagus tips, leeks and firm tomatoes

¼ cup minced onion
¼ cup oil
2 Tbs. oil

Bring the chicken stock to a boil. In a deep heavy pan saute the onion in oil. Add the millet to the onion and stir for one minute. Add ½ cups of the boiling chicken stock and stir until the liquid is absorbed. Briefly saute the chicken and add to the millet. Add 1 cup more of the stock and repeat. Add the vegetables and 1 cup more of the stock. When broth is absorbed add the rest of the stock one cup at a time until all the broth is absorbed. Add 2 Tbs. oil, mix with two forks and serve.

Dessert
Day III

Blueberry Crisp

4 cups blueberries

Nuts and seeds ground in blender
for topping

Place thawed or fresh berries into casserole dish. Top with nut and seed topping. Bake at 400°F. for about 15 minutes.

Orange Coconut Sherbet

1 Tbs. agar-agar flakes
1 cup water
1 tsp. lemon juice
1 cup orange juice
½ cup coconut
1 tsp. slippery elm

¼ cup rice syrup or sweetener (to taste)
¼ cup oil
2 cups fresh fruit (oranges, tangerines, dates)

Dissolve agar-agar flakes in water. Soak for 1 minute, then boil 1 minute, and cool 1 minute. Blend juice and coconut. Add agar-agar and remaining ingredients. Blend until smooth. Put in freezer. Serve before it gets too hard. The agar-agar does not fit in this rotation day. But it can be used if not used in the previous 3 days.

Coconut Orange Dates

¾ cup nut or seed milk
7–9 dates

¼ tsp. orange or lemon rind
(organic, unsprayed)

2 Tbs. coconut

Blend all ingredients until smooth. Pour over cooked rice and serve as is or warmed up.

Hazelnut Coconut Ice Cream

3 cups hot water
1 cup coconut
1/3 cup rice syrup or sweetener
1/3 cup safflower oil

1 Tbs. vanilla.
1 tsp. slippery elm
1/2 cup hazelnuts

Blend hot water, coconut, slippery elm and hazelnuts and strain. Add rice syrup oil and vanilla and blend again. Freeze and blend once more. Freeze a second time. It should be served before it is solidly frozen. For carob-coconut just add 3 Tbs. carob powder. Alternatively, blend the ingredients, cool them and freeze in an ice cream maker.

Fruit Pudding

1/3 cup rice flour
1/4 cup nut butter or seed meal

3 cups fruit juice

In a saucepan, combine flour and fruit juice. Cook over medium heat for 10 minutes until thickened—stir. Add nut butter and puree in blender until creamy.

Amaranth or Quinoa Pudding

2 cups cooked amaranth or quinoa
  (see page 21)

1/4 cup chopped dates
1 1/2 cups hazelnut milk (see page 26)

Mix amaranth or quinoa, dates and hazelnut milk in a deep casserole dish. Bake 20 minutes at 325. Serve hot with additional hazelnut milk.

Yeast, Milk, Wheat-Free Breakfast Day IV

If you dislike the strong flavour of dark buckwheat flour, make your own light buckwheat flour. Grind unroasted buckwheat groats in a blender for a couple of minutes, ½ cup at a time. Sieve the flour and regrind the large pieces with more groats until you have enough.

Buckwheat Arrowroot Pancakes

1½ cups light buckwheat flour
½ cup arrowroot
1½ tsp. baking soda

water as needed
3 Tbs. oil
1 egg or replacer for leavening (optional)

Mix dry with dry, wet with wet. Blend together. Add more water to make crepes. Pour onto hot skillet and cook until done.

Buckwheat Pancakes

1 cup light buckwheat flour
1 tsp. baking powder
1 cup oat flour

2 cups water
2 Tbs. oil
1 egg, well beaten or substitute for leavening (optional)

Mix dry with dry, wet with wet. Stir a little. Cook on hot skillet. Top with fruit and sweetener, e.g. maple syrup.

Oatmeal Porridge

2 cups water

1 cup oats

Cook on low heat. Sweeten and serve with seed or nut milk.

Raw-soaked Oats

Soak 1 cup oats in 2–3 cups water overnight. Serve with peaches or apricots etc. Delicious!

Plum and Pear Salad

2 cups sliced pears   3 cups plum chunks

Mix together with maple syrup or sweetener if desired. Serve with thick almond milk.

Applesauce

Peel and slice 6 apples into cooking pot. Add ½ to 1 cup water. Cook lightly for 5 minutes. Eat as is or place in blender and blend until smooth. Add ¼ tsp. cinnamon if you like.

Oat Breakfast Bars

½ cup & 2 Tbs. warm water   1 cup currants
1½ cups oat flour   ¾ cup quick rolled oats
1⅛ cup almonds or other nuts   ½ tsp. salt
   (finely chopped)

Blend water, nuts and currants together. Combine dry ingredients. Add liquid mixture to dry. Knead into stiff dough. Place on cookie sheet. Spread with hands to ¼–½" thick. Bake at 325°F. for 45 minutes.

Hot Apricot Drink

1¾ cup apple-apricot juice   2 cinnamon sticks
   (combine your own)   ¼ tsp. whole cloves

Buy apricot juice or simmer sliced apricots slowly and blend. Strain out juice. Combine juice and cloves in small saucepan. Bring to boil, then reduce heat and simmer 5 minutes. Strain into 2 mugs. Add a cinnamon stick to each. Can substitute apple-peach juice.

Prune Spread

2 cups pitted prunes　　　　　　2 cups apple juice
½ tsp. cinnamon or ⅛ tsp cloves

Simmer all ingredients in saucepan, stirring occasionally until prunes are tender and most of juice is gone. Puree when cool. Refrigerate in glass jars. Good as spread or as a filling for cookies.

Arrowroot Pancakes

1 cup nut or seed flour　　　　　1 cup water or juice
½ cup arrowroot powder　　　　1½ Tbs. oil
2 tsp. baking powder　　　　　　2 Tbs. maple syrup (optional)

In a blender mix all ingredients well. Pour onto a hot, oiled skillet and cook until done.

Oat Biscuits

1 cup oat flour, sifted　　　　　¼ cup water or juice
2½ tsp. baking powder　　　　　¼ tsp. salt
1½ Tbs. oil　　　　　　　　　　1 Tbs. maple syrup

Mix dry ingredients. Stir oil and maple syrup together and stir into flour mixture until crumbly. Add water to make a soft dough. Form dough into small biscuits and place on a greased cookie sheet. Bake at 425°F. for 15–20 minutes. Makes 8 biscuits.

Sweet Potato Muffins

1 cup mashed sweet potato　　　1 cup rolled oats
¾ cup hot water　　　　　　　　2 tsp. baking powder
½ cup chopped nuts or seeds　　2–3 Tbs. oil
2 Tbs. maple syrup

Pour hot water over oats and let soak for a few minutes. Mix the rest of the ingredients together. Place in well greased muffin tins. Bake at 400°F. for 20 minutes. Makes 18 muffins.

Fruit and Oatmeal Pudding

2 cups cooked oatmeal
½ cup chopped dried apple or
currants

½ cup seeds or chopped nuts
(optional)
1 cup diced fruit
⅓ cup juice

Combine and pour into well-oiled casserole dish. Bake at 375°F. for 15 minutes until hot.

Buckwheat Oat Pancakes

1 cup light buckwheat flour
½ cup oat flour
1½ tsp. baking powder

1¼ cup water
2 Tbs. oil
1 egg or alternative

Mix flours and baking powder. Mix remaining ingredients together and add to flour. Pour onto an oiled skillet and cook until done.

Serve with apple sauce (p. 76), cooked plums, apricot puree, or prune spread (p. 77).

Oat Waffle

1¼ oat flour
1 tsp. baking powder
¼ cup prune spread (see page 77)

1½ Tbs. oil
¾ cup water

Mix the oat flour and baking powder. Blend together the prune spread, oil and water. Stir into the flour and let sit for a couple of minutes. Pour half of the mixture into the heated waffle iron and cook till done. Makes two double waffles. If not rotating add ¼ cup soft tofu to the water and oil to make a lighter waffle.

Lunch and Dinner
Day IV

Tuna Salad

Mix a can of tuna with sliced olives or radishes and a tablespoon olive oil. Serve on oatcrackers or rolled into soft cabbage leaves. Good for a quick breakfast.

Roast Pork

Preheat oven to 450°F. Trim fat closely and place pork loin fat side up in pan. Reduce heat to 350° and cook 30–35 minutes per pound. Serve with applesauce. One pound serves 3–4.

Fish

Bake, broil or poach sole, halibut, flounder or ocean perch.

Mackerel

Tinned. Spread onto oat crackers with watercress. Good also for breakfast.

Sweet Potato—Baked

Scrub and bake at 425 for 40–60 minutes or steam until soft (about 25 minutes). Serve with cabbage salad (see below) or cooked cabbage.

Ham

Slice with apple sauce or olives on oat or buckwheat crackers (see cracker recipes).

Kasha Loaf

See casseroles—omit egg and use cabbage or broccoli rather than carrot and onion.

Red Cabbage Salad

3 Tbs. oil
1 head red cabbage, thinly sliced
1 apple, diced
3 Tbs. lemon juice (optional, or 1 tsp Vitamin C powder)

1 Tbs. maple syrup (optional)
handful of currants
1/4 tsp. allspice
2 whole cloves
dash of nutmeg (optional)

Heat oil in skillet and add cabbage. Cook, stirring until cabbage wilts. Add rest of ingredients. Cook, covered for 15 minutes at low heat.

Sweet Potato Pie

5 sweet potatoes or yams (yams are darker and sweeter)
1 1/2 cups ground almonds
1 tsp. nutmeg

1 tsp. allspice
1/4 cup maple syrup (optional)
1 tsp. cinnamon

Steam sweet potatoes until tender. Peel and mash or whip thoroughly. Add the other ingredients except almonds. Spread almonds onto pie plate, add sweet potatoes and bake at 375°F. for 40 minutes. Good hot or cold. If not rotating, add 1/2 cup pineapple chunks.

Oat Crepe

1 cup oat flour
1/2 cup arrowroot flour
2 tsp. baking powder

1 cup apple juice or water
1 1/2 Tbs. oil

Pre-heat skillet to medium heat and then lightly oil pan. Blend all the above ingredients. Pour into skillet to produce a thin even crepe. Cook 2 minutes or until top starts to dry. Flip and cook 30 seconds. Roll up with warm fruit and/or nuts for breakfast or with fish, meat or vegetable for dinner.

Buckwheat Crepe

1 cup light buckwheat flour
½ cup arrowroot flour
2 tsp. baking powder

2 cups apple juice or water
1½ Tbs. oil

Pre-heat skillet to medium heat and then lightly oil pan. Blend all the ingredients. More liquid may be needed to make a thin smooth batter. Pour into skillet to produce a thin even crepe. Cook 2 minutes or until top starts to dry. Flip and cool for 30 seconds. Roll up with warm fruit for breakfast or fish, meat or vegetables for dinner.

Mie Goreng (Indonesian noodles)

¼ lb. 100% buckwheat or 100% yam noodles
½ cup almonds, chopped
2 Tbs. oil

1 cup chopped broccoli or cauliflower
2–4 slices ginger root
1 cup finely sliced cabbage

Boil noodles until 'al dente' and drain. Yam noodles become translucent. Roast nuts in pan carefully for 3–5 minutes or use roasted nuts. Steam broccoli until slightly soft. Then sauté with cabbage and ginger until soft. Add salt if desired and add to noodles with nuts. Sauté for 3 minutes and serve hot. You can sauté pieces of any Day Four meats instead of nuts. Serves two.

Buckwheat Currant Bread

1 cup currants
1⅔ cups water or juice
½ cup oil
½ tsp. vitamin C powder
1 cup light buckwheat flour

½ cup chopped almonds
1 cup arrowroot
1 tsp. baking soda
2 tsp. cinnamon
¼ tsp. cloves

Simmer currants and water together for 10 minutes. Then add oil and vitamin C powder. Mix together the dry ingredients and add to the liquid. Pour into an 8″ square pan and bake at 400°F. for 20 minutes. Eat while warm.

Oat Bran Muffins

1 1/4 cups oat bran
1 cup oat flour
1/4 cup currants
1 tsp. baking powder
1 Tbs. arrowroot

1/4 cup chopped almonds (optional)
2 Tbs. oil
1 cup almond milk or water or juice
1/4 cup maple syrup (optional)

Heat oven to 425°F. Grease bottom only of 8 medium sized muffin cups. Combine dry ingredients. Add milk, sweetener and oil. Mix until dry ingredients are moistened. Bake 15–17 minutes. Makes 8.

Buckwheat/Arrowroot Muffins

1 1/2 cup light buckwheat flour (make in your blender)
1/2 cup arrowroot flour
2 tsp. baking powder

3/4–1/2 water or juice
1/4 cup oil
1/4 cup maple syrup (optional)

Combine flours and baking powder. Add oil, honey and water and mix with a minimum of stirring. Bake at 400°F. for 20 minutes. Makes 9.

Oat Pizza or Pie Crust

1 1/2 cup oat flour
1 tsp. baking soda

2 Tbs. oil
1/2 cup water

Combine flour and baking soda. Add oil and water. Press into oiled 8 × 12 inch pan or 2 pie plates. If dough sticks to fingers sprinkle a little flour on to dough. Add fillings and bake at 400° for about 20 minutes until crust is firm and browned.

Dessert
Day IV

Pear Crumble

28 oz. can pears (sugar-free or 2 lb.
   raw pears peeled)—drained and
   cut into 1/4" slices (save juice)
1 tsp. vanilla

2 Tbs. light oil
1 Tbs. maple syrup (optional)
1/2 cup sliced almonds

Layer the pears in an 8 x 8" pan. Combine juice of pears, vanilla and maple syrup. Drizzle over pears. Sprinkle with almonds. Drizzle oil over almonds. Bake at 350°F. for 10 minutes.

Nut-Apricot Cobbler

Soak unsulphured dried apricots until soft. Puree in blender. Serve in sherbet cups. Sprinkle with finely chopped almonds or brazil nuts.

Apple Rhubarb Crisp

Place 2–3 cups of stewed apples or pears and/or rhubarb in a casserole dish. Cover with either topping and bake for 20–30 minutes at 375°F. If you are not rotating fruit, try using blueberries or strawberries.

Topping 1: Combine
2 cups oats
1/2 cup oat flour (make in blender)
1/3 cup maple syrup (optional)
3/4 tsp. cinnamon or coriander

1/3 cup chopped almonds (optional)
1/4 cup water or juice
1/4 cup oil

Topping 2: Combine
1/2 cup light buckwheat flour
1/2 cup arrowroot flour
2 Tbs. maple syrup (optional)

3/4 tsp. cinnamon or cloves
1/3 cup chopped almonds (optional)
1/4 cup oil

Rhubarb Sauce (yield: 2 servings)

1 cup finely diced fresh rhubarb
½ cup water or juice

¼ cup maple syrup (optional) or
prune spread (page 77)

Place all ingredients in an electric blender and blend until smooth. Serve in stemmed glasses at room temperature, chilled or heated. Rhubarb is quite tart without a sweetener.

Apple Cider

3 cups apple cider
3 cloves

1 cinnamon stick

Gently simmer cider and spices. Do not allow to boil.

Fruit Jam

½ cup dried apricots
½ cup currants (or double one of above fruits)

¼ cup almonds
1¼ cups apple juice
½ cup prunes

Combine the dried fruit and juice. Soak overnight. Add to blender ½ at a time. Puree.

Apricot Muffins

1½ cup apricot puree (see recipe)
2 cup oat or buckwheat flour
2 tsp. baking powder

½ cup pitted prunes
¼ cup oil
¼ cup chopped prunes
(optional)

Wash, slice and remove stone from apricots. Puree in a blender until smooth. Add a little water to a heavy pot and cook until slightly thick. Mix flour and baking powder. Add prunes, oil and apricot puree to blender and blend until smooth. Add prunes if desired. Spoon batter into well-oiled muffin tins. Bake at 350 for 20 minutes. Makes 10. Makes a heavy muffin. If not rotating add one egg to recipe.

Yeast, Milk and Wheat-Free Baking

These recipes do not fit into a rotation plan exactly.

Date Oatmeal Cake

Sift together into a bowl:

½ cup oat flour
1 tsp. cinnamon

1 tsp. cloves
1 tsp. baking powder

Pour 1 cup boiling water over 2 cups rolled oats, mix well, cool slightly, then blend in:

½ cup oil
2 eggs or alternative for binding

1 cup coarsely chopped walnuts
1½ cups finely chopped dates

Pour oatmeal mixture into dry ingredients and mix well. Bake in an 8″ square pan at 350°F. for 45 minutes or until done.

Millet Apple Cake

⅓ cup vegetable shortening or butter
2 eggs
¼ cup sweetener
1 tsp. vanilla
½ tsp. nutmeg
¼ tsp. cinnamon
1½ cups millet flour

¼ cup rice flour
3 tsp. baking powder
½ salt
½ cup chopped nuts
½ cup chopped raisins
1 cup apple juice

Cream shortening, eggs, sweetener, and vanilla. Combine these with dry ingredients and gradually add apple juice. Beat until smooth. Pour into oiled 9″ cake pan and bake at 375°F. for 25–30 minutes or until done.

Carob Nut Log

½ cup carob powder
½ cup ground mixed nuts
½ cup sesame seeds
½ cup pecans or large walnut pieces
¼ cup honey

2 Tbs. unrefined oil
½ cup unhulled sunflower seeds
½ cup soy flour or other flour
½ cup water if needed

Combine all ingredients and mix thoroughly. Refrigerate. When it is fully chilled, oil your hands and scrape the mixture into a log or roll into small balls. roll the log in additional finely chopped seeds or nuts until well coated. Store, covered, in refrigerator. Slice to serve. The flavour is best after a few days' refrigeration. The log will keep for weeks.

Tofu Cheesecake

Filling:
2 lbs. soft tofu
1/4 cup pineapple juice
1/2 cup oil
2 tsp. vanilla
1 banana

Crust:
2 cups coconut or 1 1/2 cups
   coconut and 1/2 cup ground
   roasted or raw nuts and seeds.

Mix crust ingredients together and press into large pie plate. Combine all filling ingredients in blender and blend until creamy (2 batches might be easier). Pour filling into crust and bake at 350°F. for 40 minutes or until top is golden brown and cake has jelled. Serve chilled with fruit if desired. A full recipe will fit into a pie plate with 7 inch bottom.

Hazelnut Cake

2 cups shelled hazelnuts   2 large eggs
½ cup raisin pudding

Grind hazelnuts into flour in a blender. Mix with raisin pudding. Beat eggs until light and frothy. Gently mix with hazelnuts. Pour into a greased 8 inch pan. Bake at 350F for 35-4 minutes. Allow to cool before serving.

Oat Pancakes

3 cups rolled oats   ¾ cup oat, barley or tapioca flour
3 eggs beaten or substitute for   1 Tbs. sweetener
   binding

Soak rolled oats in 1 pint water for 3 hours. Add eggs, sweetener and flour. Drop small pancakes in drying pan with heated oil and fry until crisp on both sides.

Oat and Apple Pancakes

1½ cups rolled oats   1 cup water, nut or soy
1½ tsp. ground almonds   milk
pinch of salt   2 egg yolks
1 lb. grated apples   2 stiffly beaten egg whites

Mix oats with water and let stand for one hour. Add the egg yolks and whites, almonds and salt. Fold the apples into the batter. Spoon batter into a little hot oil in a frying pan. Serve with maple syrup and cinnamon.

Blueberry Pancakes

1 cup blueberries—fresh or frozen
2 cups liquid—soy milk, juice,
    water
1 tsp. baking soda
1 tsp. baking powder

2 Tbs. oil
2 cups flour, e.g. 1 cup buckwheat,
    ½ cup soy, ½ cup rice
2 tsp. flax seed
½ cup water

Simmer flax seed in ½ cup water for 10 minutes; cool. Sift dry ingredients, combine wet ingredients, then add wet to dry ingredients. Add blueberries and cook.

Rice Pancakes

2 cups rice flour
½ tsp. baking soda
1 egg or ½ cup tofu
1 tsp. baking powder
¼ cup oil

1½ cups soy milk or other milk
    substitute with 2 tsp. vinegar or
    lemon juice)
1 Tbs. honey
¼ tsp. salt

Combine everything except the rice flour until smooth. Add rice flour and blend until smooth. Cook in lightly oiled pan. Make small 4″ pancakes.

Oat Bran Muffins

2¼ cups oat bran cereal
¼ cup raisins or other dried fruit
¾ cup milk or alternative
¼ cup honey or maple syrup
1 Tbs. baking powder

2 beaten eggs or egg replacer for
    binding
¼ cup chopped nuts (optional)
¼ cup chopped nuts (optional)
¼ tsp. salt
2 Tbs. vegetable oil

Heat oven to 425°F. Grease bottom only of 12 medium sized muffin cups. Combine dry ingredients. Add milk, eggs, honey and oil. Mix until dry ingredients are moistened. Fill muffin tins ¾ full. Bake 15–17 minutes.

Brown Rice Muffins

2 cups brown rice flour
2 tsp. baking powder
¾ cup milk alternative

1 Tbs. oil
4 Tbs. corn syrup or honey
1 egg or substitute for binding

Sift all dry ingredients together. Add milk, molasses and oil. Beat egg and add to mixture. Mix until smooth. Pour into oiled muffin pan. Fill ¾ full. Bake at 375°F. for 20–25 minutes. For variety add ¼ cup sunflower seeds, ¼ cup sesame seeds, ¼ cup chopped nuts or ⅓ cup raisins to dry ingredients. Makes 6.

Soy Muffins

1½ cups soy flour
2 tsp. baking powder
¼ tsp. salt
2 egg yolks
3 Tbs. sweetener
1 Tbs. oil

1 cup soy or nut milk
¼ cup raisins
¼ cup chopped nuts (optional)
2 egg whites (beaten)

Mix together the soy flour, baking powder and salt. Cream the egg yolks with the sweetener and oil. Slowly add milk and pour into dry ingredients. Add nuts and raisins. Fold in stiff egg whites. pour into oiled muffin tins and bake at 375°F. for 30 minutes. Very heavy.

Fruit Muffins

1–1½ cups pear or apple juice
¼ cup honey
1 egg or substitute for binding
2 Tbs. oil

2 tsp. baking powder
½ tsp. cinnamon
1½ cups oat flour or rice flour
1 cup chopped almonds (optional)

Mix fruit juice, honey, oil and eggs together. Add the other ingredients and mix well. Oil and flour a muffin tin. Bake at 350°F. for 20 minutes. Allow to cool.

Pie Crust from Rice Flour

Mix in a bowl:

2 cups rice flour or flakes   ½ tsp. cinnamon
½ cup vegetable shortening, or
margarine—melted

Pat mixture evenly in a 9″ square pan. Bake 10 minutes in a hot oven.

Banana Pie

½ cup dates   ½ cup coconut
½ cup seeds or filberts   4 bananas
2½ cups water   1 tsp vanilla
½ cup arrowroot powder

Liquify nuts and dates in blender with water. Slowly while stirring, add liquid to arrowroot. Heat and stir until it thickens. Mash 2 bananas and add along with vanilla. Slice 2 bananas into bottom of pie dish, sprinkle coconut over bananas, cover with filling and chill.

Strawberry Torte

2 Tbs. honey   ½ cup tofu
1 cup whole strawberries   8 oz. can crushed pineapple (water
nutmeg   packed)

Crush strawberries. Whip tofu and add all other ingredients. Mix until smooth; refrigerate; garnish with nutmeg and serve.

Peach Cream Pie

2½ cups sliced peaches or other fruit   ¼ cup sesame butter or ground nuts
1 tsp oil   2 Tbs. arrowroot powder
1 Tbs. sweetener   coconut
1 cup water

Heat oil and saute peaches. Mix sweetener, sesame butter, and water well. Raise to a boil and add arrowroot. Cook 3 minutes. Add peaches. Sprinkle a thick layer of coconut onto pie plate. Pour in filling and chill.

Strawberry Flan

1 tsp. vanilla
1/4 cup tapioca flour
1 1/4 cups soy milk

3 eggs
2 Tbs. honey or sweetener

Beat the eggs, honey, tapioca and vanilla together. Scald the soy milk and add to egg mixture. Stir and cook in a double boiler over rapidly boiling water for 12 minutes stirring to prevent lumps. Tapioca will thicken as it cools. Pour into pie shell, cool and top with sliced strawberries.

Crust: Mix together 1 cup coconut and 2 Tbs. melted margarine and pat onto the bottom of a pie plate. Bake at 350°F. for 10 minutes.

Pumpkin Pie

2 eggs or 1/4 cup tofu
2 cups pumpkin puree
3/4 cups soy milk
2 Tbs. molasses
2 Tbs. honey

coconut or ground nuts
1/2 tsp. ginger
1/4 tsp. cloves
3/4 tsp. nutmeg
1/2 tsp. cinnamon

Put all ingredients in blender and blend until combined. Sprinkle coconut or nuts onto pie plate thickly. Pour onto coconut pie crust and bake at 425°F. for 15 minutes. Lower to 350°F. and bake 1/2 hour more.

Banana Bread #1—rice, soy flour

1 cup rice flour
1/2 cup soy flour
2 Tbs. tapioca flour
2 tsp. baking powder
2 eggs

2 ripe bananas
1/4 cup oil
1/4 cup sweetener
1/4 tsp. salt

Mix rice, soy and tapioca flours with baking soda and salt. Blend bananas, oil, sweetener and eggs. Mix into dry ingredients. Bake at 350°F. for 45 minutes in 4" x 8" bread pan.

Banana Bread #2—amaranth flour

Mix 1 cup amaranth flour and ½ cup tapioca flour and 2 tsp. baking powder. Proceed as for banana bread #1 substituting these flours.

Gingerbread

1¼ cup rice flour
1½ cup corn starch
1 tsp. baking soda
1 tsp. cinnamon
¼ tsp. clove

¼ tsp. ginger
⅓ cup molasses or sweetener
½ cup oil
1 cup boiling water
2 eggs—well beaten

Mix dry ingredients. Add molasses, oil and then water. Add eggs. Bake at 325°F. for 45 minutes in 9 × 9 inch pan. If you like add ⅓ cup of raisins or chopped nuts.

Quick Bread

⅔ cup rice flour
⅓ cup potato flour
½ cup oat bran
½ cup chopped raisins or other dried
fruit
½ tsp. cinnamon

1 tsp. vanilla
2 tsp. baking soda
1 cup nut or soy milk
1 egg or replacer for binding
1 mashed banana or ½ cup apricots
 or pumpkin

Combine flours, oat bran, raisins, cinnamon and baking soda. Combine nut milk, egg, oil, banana and vanilla. Then mix contents of both bowls together. Pour one cup of batter into each of three well-oiled soup cans. Cover with foil and steam them on a rack in a large covered pot for one hour. Let loaves cool before slicing. The loaves will keep for about one week if wrapped in plastic and refrigerated.

Zucchini Bread

3 cups grated zucchini
2 eggs
½ cup brown sugar or honey
(optional)
3 tsp. vanilla
1½ cups soy flour
1½ cups rice flour

1 tsp. pumpkin spice
½ tsp. baking soda
½ tsp. baking powder
1 cup chopped walnuts
3 Tbs. oil

Beat eggs, blend in sugar and add zucchini, oil and vanilla. Combine dry ingredients and add to wet ingredients. Pour into 2 small loaf tins or an 8″ x 10″ pan. Bake at 325°F. for 45 minutes.

Carob Tofu Pudding—no cooking

2 Tbs. carob powder
20 oz. soft tofu
2 Tbs. tahini (sesame seed paste)
2–3 Tbs. lemon juice

1½ tsp. vanilla
½ tsp. cinnamon
¼ cup honey

Add ingredients to bowl or blender. Whip or blend until light and fluffy. Put in serving bowls and chill until set. (If you can wait that long!)

Fruit and Nut Crumble

4 portions stewed fruit (½ to 1 cup
    per person) e.g. apples,
    blueberries, pears, apricots,
    berries, dates, peaches,
    separately or combined.

4 Tbs. honey
1 cup chopped nuts and/or seeds
2 Tbs. oil
4 Tbs. water

Mix oil, honey, water, and nuts. Spread half in the bottom of a casserole dish. Add fruit and top with remaining mixture. Bake at 400°F. for about 15 minutes.

Puffed Grain Squares

½ cup nut butter (peanut, sesame, etc.)

¼ cup honey

3 cups puffed rice, millet or corn

¼ cup vegetable shortening, or margarine

½ cup carob chips (check ingredients) or ⅓ cup carob powder

Melt nut butter, margarine, honey and carob together. Mix in the puffed grain. Stir well until grain is coated. Place in 6″ x 6″ pan. Refrigerate.

Peanut Butter Squares

¼ cup honey

¼ cup peanut butter

½ tsp. salt

12 oz. tofu

2 tsp. vanilla

2 eggs

Blend all of the above and spread into a flat layer in an 8″ x 8″ pan.

⅓ cup honey

⅓ cup carob powder

2 tsp. vanilla

Stir together and pour on to of first layer. Marbilize the layers with a knife. Freeze and enjoy.

Yeast, Milk and Wheat-Free Dips, Sauces, Gravies, and Dressings

Baba Ghannouj (Eggplant Sesame Paste Dip)

1 large or 2 small eggplants

Cut off the tip of the eggplant. Bake at 350°F. for 20–30 minutes until soft all over and partly collapsed. Cool. Remove skin. Place in bowl. Mash with fork, foodmill or electric egg beater until smooth paste. Add:

⅓ cup lemon juice
3–4 Tbs. stock or water
6 Tbs. tahini

2–3 large cloves of garlic (crushed or minced)
½ tsp. salt (optional)

Mix to a smooth paste. Add liquid as needed for dip consistency. Chill 2–3 hours or overnight.

Topping:
2 Tbs. olive oil
1 sprig parsley

¼ tsp. chili pepper

Serve with green peppers, carrots, celery or other crisp vegetables.

Humus (Chick pea-Sesame Paste Dip)

1 cup chick peas (garbanzo)   *4 cups water*

Cover chick peas with water. Soak overnight to reduce cooking time. Boil in heavy saucepan over high heat. Cover. Reduce heat to medium low. Simmer until tender. Drain. (Reserve stock for later use.) Mash with foodmill, fork or fingers (not blender) ½ cup at a time. Add:

⅓ lemon juice
¼ cup tahini (sesame butter)
1 tsp. salt
¼-½ tsp. hot chili powder
1 large sprig parsley

⅔ large garlic cloves, crushed or
    minced
⅓ cup chick pea stock or water
2 Tbs. olive or vegetable oil

Mix to smooth paste. Should have dip consistency. Chill 2–3 hours or overnight.

Topping: *2 Tbs. oil; ¼–½ tsp. chili pepper; 1 large sprig parsley*

Vegetable Walnut Pate

1½ cups green beans
2 eggs
¼ cup toasted walnuts

2 Tbs. mayonnaise
½ cup finely minced onion
2 Tbs. dry white wine (if tolerated)

Blend separately green beans and walnuts. Saute the onion. Combine and mix finely all the ingredients. Season with salt, pepper, and nutmeg as desired.

Sesame Salad Dressing

¼ cup tahini
1 tsp. kelp
½ clove garlic, finely chopped

juice of ½ lemon
water (to thin dressing)

Combine tahini with kelp, garlic and lemon juice. Add a few tablespoons water to thin to desired thickness. Mix until smooth. For mock tuna spread, add ½ cup chopped onion, ½ cup chopped celery, and ½ cup mixed alfalfa, mung and lentil sprouts. Blend until smooth.

Sesame Butter Dressing (yield ½ cup)

¼ cup sesame butter (tahini) 3 Tbs. lemon juice
h1 tsp. grated onion ¼ tsp. salt
h1 tsp. chervil or ¼ tsp. tarragon or 1 Tbs. olive oil
 1 tsp. basil

Mix well. Serve over Spring Dandelion Salad or other salads.

Garlic Dill Dressing (yield 1½ cups)

½ lb. fresh tofu, drained, sliced 3 Tbs. lemon juice
2 Tbs. oil 1 tsp. garlic salt
4 tsp. dill seed or ⅛ tsp. anise

Blend all ingredients in blender—add a spoonful of water if necessary.
Toss with salads or over fresh vegetables. Use in place of mayonnaise.

Sunflower Dressing (topping for potatoes)

1⅓ cups sunflower seeds ½ tsp. onion powder or 1 Tbs.
1 tsp. salt minced onion
¼ tsp. garlic powder or 1 minced 1⅔ cups water
garlic clove ⅓ cup lemon juice (to taste)

Blend all ingredients. Excellent with avocado or tomato.

Oil and Lemon Juice Dressing

3 Tbs. lemon juice 2 cloves of garlic—minced
1 Tbs. mustard (optional)   (optional)
 ½ cup olive oil

Mix lemon juice with mustard and garlic if tolerated. Slowly add oil
while stirring until oil is well blended.

Fish Sauces

(1) Ginger Sauce: Simmer ¼ cup oil (or butter) with juice and finely grated peel of 1 orange, 1 tsp. grated fresh ginger and 1 small clove of garlic for 5 minutes.

(2) Herb Sauce: Blend ¼ cup olive oil with 1 tsp. Dijon mustard, 1 Tbs. lemon juice and pinch of cayenne. Add 1 Tbs. chopped fresh dill or tarragon.

(3) Tomato Caper Sauce

28 oz. canned tomatoes	1 Tbs. capers
2 cloves garlic	¼ tsp. oregano
¼ tsp basil	

Puree or chop drained tomatoes. Simmer in a saucepan with crushed garlic, drained capers and oregano and basil until it begins to thicken slightly.

Top broiled or baked fish with one of the above.

Cranberry Sauce

1 cup orange juice	½–1 cup cooked cranberries
1 small unpeeled apple sliced	1–2 Tbs. honey

Blend together the juice, apples and honey. Add the cranberries until the mixture thickens.

Nut Gravies

2 cups of cashew milk (or any nut or seed milk—see dairy alternatives)	2 Tbs. oil (optional)
	2 Tbs. arrowroot powder
2 Tbs. chopped onion	pinch of sea salt

Season with pinch of either basil, thyme, dill, celery seed powder, garlic, cayenne or black pepper. Simmer in saucepan until thick. ½ cup of chopped parsley, chives, leeks or alfalfa sprouts may be added prior to serving.

Soy Mayonnaise

½ cup soy milk or cashew milk
⅔ cup soy oil
¼ tsp. salt
½ tsp. onion powder

¼ tsp. celery seed
1 tsp. honey
½ tsp. paprika
Tbs. lemon juice

Blend milk and seasonings together. Gradually add oil, very slowly until it becomes thick. Lastly stir in the lemon juice.

Tofu Mayonnaise

1 cup tofu (6½ oz)
2 Tbs. chopped onion
3 Tbs. lemon juice

paprika to taste or dill, or touch of
    mustard or cayenne
1 tsp. honey
¼ cup oil

Blend all ingredients except oil and lemon juice. Add oil very slowly while continuing to blend. Add lemon juice, blend 10 seconds more.

Good as a dip as well.

Tahini and Honey Syrup

¼ cup honey   ¼ cup tahini

Blend honey and tahini. Add water until it reaches desired thickness. ½ tsp. vanilla is optional. Serve on fruit salad or grains as thick sauce or thin syrup.

Wheat, Yeast and Milk Free Soups

Bean Soup

3½ cups water
3 chopped tomatoes or 2 Tbs.
  tomato pureé
1½ cups cooked or canned beans

chopped vegetables (see
  instructions)
seasoning herbs

Put water into a heavy saucepan. Add chopped vegetables, e.g. onion, celery, carrots, parsley, turnip, potatoes, tomatoes or tomato paste—seasoning of your choice, i.e. cayenne pepper, basil, sea salt. Simmer for 15 minutes. Add cooked beans, e.g. lima, navy, black, soy, pinto, or romano. Simmer an additional 10 minutes.

Split Pea Soup (serves 3–4)

1 cup dry split peas
4 cups water
1 small onion
1 carrot

parsley
¼ tsp. chervil
½ tsp. savory

Combine the peas, water and onion and simmer for 45 minutes. Add chopped carrot and parsley and cook 15 minutes longer.

Lentil Soup

1½ cups lentils, washed
1½ quarts cold water
2 Tbs. olive oil
3 cloves garlic, chopped
1 stalk celery, chopped
fresh ground black pepper

1 onion, chopped fine
¼ cup celery leaves, chopped
⅓ cup raw brown rice
2 Tbs. tomato paste
2 Tbs. parsley, chopped

In heavy pot, heat oil. Add chopped vegies and rice. Cook, stirring 5 minutes. Add lentils and water. Bring to a boil, cover and simmer 1½–2 hours. (You can add millet in place of rice). During the last 15 minutes, add chopped kale, escarole or spinach. You can mix 1 cup lentils with ½ cup split peas.

Vegetable Soup

2–3 Tbs. oil
1 onion chopped (optional)
4 potatoes scrubbed and diced or 3
    sweet potatoes peeled and diced
4 cups tomato juice, or 3 Tbs.
    tomato paste (keep the unused
    portion frozen)

1 cup chopped parsley or chives
4 carrots thinly sliced
2 turnips diced
1/4 head cabbage, shredded or
    chopped
1/4 head cabbage, shredded or
    chopped

Heat oil and saute onion until tender (if using tomato paste, add now and saute). Add potatoes, carrots, turnips, cabbage and 1/2–1 cup water to cover. Simmer until potatoes and turnip are tender, about 1/2 hour. Add the tomato juice (or 4 cups water) and continue cooking until heated. Add the chopped parsley or chives and serve.

Sesame Cream of Tomato Soup

2 cups fresh tomato puree
1 small onion, chopped
1/2 tsp. basil
1 tsp. honey

2 cups rich sesame milk
1 small garlic clove, minced
1 tsp. salt

Add onion, garlic and seasonings to tomato puree. Blend. Add sesame milk to blend. Warm—do not boil.

Wheat, Yeast and Milk Free Casseroles

Yam/Sweet Potato Pie

2 lb. yams or sweet potato
1 cup canned unsweetened
   pineapple
2 Tbs. lemon juice

¼ cup raisins (optional)
½ tsp. cinnamon
½ tsp. cinnamon (optional)

Steam yams until soft and peel. Mash to fine texture with other ingredients. Serve cold or reheat covered in oven.

Kasha Loaf (buckwheat groats)

2¾ cups water
½ cup grated carrot
1⅓ cups kasha
½ cup oat flour

paprika
1 Tbs. chopped onion
1 clove minced onion
1 egg—beaten

Saute onion and garlic in oil. Boil the water, then add carrots, kasha, onion and garlic. Cover. Reduce heat and cook for 20 minutes. Mix in the egg and flour. Pour into an oiled casserole and bake 30 minutes at 350°F. Serve with hot tomato sauce or nut gravy, sprinkled with paprika.

Tofu Casserole

1 lb. soft tofu cut in ½" cubes
½ cup peas
1 zucchini, thinly sliced
½ tsp. kelp, dulse or salt (optional)

1 cup tomato sauce
1 onion, chopped
1 clove garlic, chopped

Sauté tofu, zucchini, onion and garlic. Place in casserole and pour on the tomato sauce. Cover and cook at 375°F. for 20 minutes.

Indian Pudding

Prepare the night before for a filling breakfast or serve as a dessert.

2½ cups sesame milk or soy milk or juice

½ cup cornmeal

1 large egg, beaten lightly or ¼ cup tofu

3 Tbs. light brown sugar (optional)

3 Tbs. maple syrup (optional)

3 Granny Smith apples, chopped

¼ cup unsulphured dark molasses

¼ tsp. ground ginger

¼ tsp. nutmeg

½ tsp. cinnamon

½ cup raisins

In a large saucepan, scald milk, then stir in cornmeal. Stir and cook for 2 minutes. Remove from heat and add egg. Stir in sugar and maple syrup and molasses. Then add ginger, nutmeg, cinnamon, salt, apples, and raisins. Mix well. Turn into well oiled casserole (1½ quart). Bake at 325°F. for 50 minutes to 1 hour. Dust with cinnamon.

Chick Pea Patties

2 tins chick peas—drained

2 Tbs. green pepper

2 Tbs. red pepper

1 Tbs. onion

2 Tbs. Tahini

1 clove garlic

seasonings

¼ cup ground sunflower seeds

Mash chick peas with potato masher. Add chopped up vegetables, sunflower seeds, tahini and seasonings (also one egg if desired). Mix well. Form into patties and bake at 350°F. for ½ hour. Top with spicy tomato sauce, chutney or nut gravies.

Millet Casserole

1 cup washed millet

3½ cups water or soy milk

2 Tbs. oil

cinnamon

sweetener or chopped fruit

Bring water or soy milk to a boil. Add washed millet and a dash of salt and simmer for 35–45 minutes. Add oil and cool. Then spread mixture on cookie sheet and sprinkle with sweetener or chopped fruit and cinnamon. Bake for 20 minutes in a hot oven. Serve with apple sauce or stewed fruit.

Wheat, Yeast and Milk Free Crackers and Flat Breads

Yuca/Cassava Pancakes with Chives or Parsley

*1 lb. fresh yuca or cassava, peeled
or frozen, thawed
2 Tbs. chopped fresh chives or
parsley
salt and pepper to taste*

*6 Tbs. oil
½ cup fresh ground hazelnuts (make
in blender)
1 egg beaten to blend*

Boil cassava until easily pierced with fork—about 35 minutes. Drain well. Puree in processor. Press through coarse sieve into bowl. Stir in chives, then egg. Season generously with salt and pepper. Form 3 inch patties—½ inch thick. Coat completely with hazelnuts, shake off excess. Heat oil in preheated heavy medium skillet over medium–high heat. Add patties and cook on both sides until golden brown—about 5 minutes. Remove using slotted spatula and drain on towels. Serve hot. Makes four servings.

Corn-Oat Skillet Bread

*¾ cup rolled oats
¼ cup yellow corn meal
1½ tsp. baking powder
½ tsp. baking soda
1 cup liquid (water, soy milk)*

*⅓ cup minced scallion
2 Tbs. minced parsley leaves
3 Tbs. oil
pinch of cayenne*

In a bowl, combine the dry ingredients. Add the wet ingredients and let stand ten minutes. In a heavy oven proof skillet 7–8 inches across the bottom heat 2 Tbs. of oil on moderate–high element till hot, add batter, spread it evenly and drizzle remaining oil over it. Bake the bread in the middle of the hot oven for 15 minutes. Invert a large plate over the skillet and invert the bread onto it. Slide the bread back into the skillet bake again for 10 minutes or until underside is brown. Let bread cool for 5 minutes—cut into wedges.

You can use combinations of other flours, e.g. chick pea and oat.

Chick Pea Skillet Bread

1 cup chick pea flour
1½ tsp. baking powder
3 Tbs. oil
1 cup water

Any of the following: ⅓ cup minced
scallion, 2 Tbs. parsley, 1 tsp.
fresh chopped basil, ½ tsp.
rosemary or oregano

In a bowl combine the dry ingredients. Add liquid and herbs. Let stand for 15 minutes. In a heavy oven proof skillet 7–8 inches bottom diameter—heat 2 Tbs. oil over moderate to high heat—add batter. Spread evenly. Drizzle remaining oil over it. Bake in pre-heated oven—400°F.—15 minutes. Invert a large plate over the skillet and invert the bread onto it. Slide it back into skillet and bake for 10 minutes more or until brown.

Crackers

1½ cups oat flour
1 Tbs. oil
pinch baking powder

1 cup water
pinch salt

Pre-heat oven to 325°F. Pour into 7 x 11 pan. Spread to even layer. Bake 20 minutes and then cut into squares. Bake for another 20 minutes.

Experiment to find your favourite type of cracker by using light buckwheat flour, chickpea flour or others. They can be topped with poppy or sesame seeds.

Hotcakes

1 cup soya flour
1 Tbs. oil
4 to 6 oz. water

pinch baking powder
1 cup corn flour
pinch salt

Mix dry ingredients, add oil and water and blend. Use 1 tsp. oil to cook each in small griddle. Makes about 4.

Wheat, Yeast and Milk Free
Ice Cream

These recipes use the Donvier Ice Cream Maker. This is an inexpensive ice cream maker that does not require salt or ice but uses a reusable cylinder that you freeze overnight. These recipes will work with any ice cream maker. If an ice cream maker is unavailable, carefully blend tofu and frozen berries from Berry Ice Cream recipe. The berries will partly freeze the tofu creating a delightful soft ice cream.

Use soft tofu if you can find it. Other tofus will have a stronger soy flavour.

Berry Ice Cream

10 oz. soft tofu
1/4 cup fruit juice or sweetener
(optional)

10 oz. raspberries, blueberries, or
    strawberries etc. (fresh/frozen)

Blend all the ingredients thoroughly and place in ice cream maker. Follow your specific machine's directions for making ice cream.

Carob Ice Cream

10 oz. soft tofu
1/2 tsp. vanilla
1/8 cup unsweetened carob chips
(optional)

1/4 cup carob powder
1/4 cup sweetener (optional)

Blend all ingredients together except carob chips and place in ice cream maker. Add carob chips halfway through freezing process.

Pineapple Ice Cream

¾ cup crushed pineapple (in its own juice)

½ cup pineapple juice (unsweetened)

½ cup apple or other fruit juice

1 egg white beaten till foamy (optional)

Add pineapple and juices to egg white. Place in ice cream maker. Follow machine directions for making ice cream. Ice cream can be topped with chopped nuts, coconut, granola, etc.

Wheat, Yeast and Milk Free Snacks

Day One
Peanuts
Sunflower Seeds
Cashews
Pistachios
Figs
Bananas
Chamomile Tea
Pineapple Juice
Peanut/Cashew Butter Cookies
Poppy Banana Bread
Tofu Yogurt (page 48)
Cucumber

Day Two
Walnuts
Pecans
Grapes
Berries
Dried Papaya
Mint Tea
Grape Juice
Papaya Juice
Tomato Juice
Corn Bread
Raisin Pudding
Popcorn
Corn Chips (page 60)

Day Three
Filberts
Dates
Orange
Tangerine
Wintergreen Tea
Citrus juice
Rice cakes
Rice Crackers
Carrot Bread
Amaranth Muffin
Carrot Sticks
Celery Sticks

Day Four
Almonds
Brazil Nuts
Roasted chestnuts
Dried or fresh apple
Pear—dried or fresh
Prunes
Peaches
Cherries
Oat cakes
Ginger tea
Apple juice
Rose hip tea

FOOD SOURCES

Agar-Agar	Natural food stores, Oriental food stores
Amaranth	Natural food stores
Biscuits: rice, corn	Specialty food departments
Breads	Specialty bakeries, natural food stores
Carob	Natural food stores
Carrot Juice (fresh)	Natural food stores
Chicken (chemically less contaminated)	Natural food stores
Coffee: chicory, dahlia, grain	Natural food stores, supermarkets
Eggs: (chemically less contaminated) Duck, Quail	Natural food stores, farmer's markets, try university agriculture colleges
Fish (unusual)	Oriental fish stores, frozen fish displays
Flours: oat, rice, buckwheat, glutinous (sweet) rice, millet, potato, soy, chickpea, peanut, etc.	Natural food stores, Chinese, Japanese grocers, East Indian grocers
Fruits	Chinese, Japanese green grocers, (unusual), Natural food stores(chemically less contaminated)
Ice Cream: soy, rice	Natural food stores
Lecithin Spread	Natural food stores
Meat: Buffalo, venison, goat	Specialty food stores, ethnic grocers and meat stores
Millet	Natural food stores
Noodles: bean starch, buckwheat, corn, rice	Natural food stores, Chinese and Japanese grocers
Nut butters: almond, cashew etc.	Natural food stores—raw or roasted
Oat cakes	Delicatessen, supermarket
Puffed rice, corn, oat, millet	Natural food stores, supermarkets
Quinoa	Natural food stores
Rice cakes and crackers	Natural food stores, supermarkets
Rice muffins	Specialty bakeries, natural food stores
Seaweed	Japanese stores, Natural food stores
Soy mayonnaise	Natural food stores
Soy milk	Natural food stores, Chinese grocers
Tahini	Middle eastern food stores, Natural food stores
Tofu	Natural food stores, supermarket, Chinese and Japanese grocers
Vegetables Unusual ie. taro, cassava, malanga	Chinese grocers; chemically less contaminated —Natural food stores, farmer's market
Wine	no additives or sulphites—San Lazlo—from the Okanagan valley, B.C., Canada

Index

ORDER FORM

Please rush me_____copies of FREEDOM FROM ALLERGY COOKBOOK. $11.95 per copy. In Canada add GST 84¢ per copy.

For postage and handling, add $2.00 for the first book and 50¢ for each additional book.

☐   I can't wait 3-4 weeks for Book Rate. Instead here's $3.00 per copy for Air Mail.

Total enclosed $ _____

☐   Cheque   ☐   Money Order

Sorry, credit orders not accepted.

Mail order to:
BLUE POPPY PRESS
212–2678 W. Broadway
Vancouver, B.C.
V6K 2G3

Bulk purchase inquiries invited.

Name_____

Address_____

City_____

Prov./State_____

Zip/Postal Code_____

Telephone (_____)_____

ORDER FORM

Please rush me_____copies of FREEDOM FROM ALLERGY COOKBOOK. $11.95 per copy. In Canada add GST 84¢ per copy.

For postage and handling, add $2.00 for the first book and 50¢ for each additional book.

☐   I can't wait 3-4 weeks for Book Rate. Instead here's $3.00 per copy for Air Mail.

Total enclosed $ _____

☐   Cheque   ☐   Money Order

Sorry, credit orders not accepted.

Mail order to:
BLUE POPPY PRESS
212–2678 W. Broadway
Vancouver, B.C.
V6K 2G3

Bulk purchase inquiries invited.

Name_____

Address_____

City_____

Prov./State_____

Zip/Postal Code_____

Telephone (_____)_____